W9-AUE-138

Online Marketing Simulations

The Definitive Methodology For Predicting The Future Of Your Online Business

Kevin Hillstrom

Acknowledgements

I would like to acknowledge Jim Fulton, President of Customer Metrics, for pioneering much of the work that ultimately led to the creation of Multichannel Forensics, and finally, Online Marketing Simulations (OMS).

Copyright © 2009 by Kevin Hillstrom

All rights reserved. No part of this publication may be reproduced or transmitted in any form or by any means, electronic or mechanical, including photocopy, recording, email, Internet, or any information storage and retrieval system now known or to be invented, without permission in writing from the author.

13 Digit ISBN: 978-1-4495-4396-9

Published in the United States of America by Kevin Hillstrom

To order books:
http://amazon.com

Manufactured in the United States of America
First Edition

Cover Design: Kevin Hillstrom and Createspace.com
Cover Art: Tori Benz-Hillstrom and http://istockphoto.com

Table of Contents

Biography

Kevin Hillstrom is a database marketing veteran with more than twenty years of experience analyzing customer behavior at many of America's greatest multichannel retailers.

Kevin began his professional career in 1998 as a Statistical Analyst at the Garst Seed Company, analyzing corn and sorghum trials.

In 1990, Kevin became a Statistical Analyst at Lands' End. It was at Lands' End where Kevin learned many of the tricks and techniques required to effectively model customer behavior. Kevin worked with a very bright direct marketing team, developing experiments that explained how customers interacted with different catalog titles over time, learning all about the ways that cannibalization of marketing activities erode company profitability. Kevin ended his tenure at Lands' End in late 1995, as Manager of Analytical Services.

In 1995, Kevin became Manager of Analytical Services at Eddie Bauer. Working with an integrated database (retail, catalog, online transactions), Kevin was able to demonstrate how customer behavior changed when new stores were opened in new markets, and how customer behavior changed when new stores were opened in existing markets. As Director of Circulation, Kevin partnered with a seasoned team of Executives to deliver the most profit ever generated by the direct-to-consumer division (catalog + internet), by reducing promotions (free shipping, % off offers), reducing catalog advertising to retail and online customers, and by using advanced statistical models to target customers with appropriate direct mail offerings. It was at Eddie Bauer that Kevin developed the methodologies that would ultimately become the foundation of "Multichannel Forensics".

Following a nine month stint as a Sr. Consultant at Avenue A, Kevin became Vice President of Direct Marketing at Nordstrom. The Executive team at Nordstrom Direct was charged with turning around a business that generated more than $300,000,000 in annual sales, but was losing more than $30,000,000 in profit each year. Within just two years, Kevin and his Executive team partners were able to re-calibrate catalog contact strategies and online marketing activities, bringing the business back to break-even.

In 2003, Kevin became Vice President of Database Marketing, working in the corporate office. Kevin's team was asked to integrate outbound customer marketing strategies (direct mail, catalogs, e-mail marketing), using an integrated transactional database. In 2004, Kevin was part of a team that decided to eliminate traditional catalog marketing, a decision that was widely criticized by purveyors of existing marketing best practices. In fact, Kevin was skeptical, too. However, within twelve months of eliminating a traditional catalog marketing program, retail comp store sales continued to increase, and without the support of catalog marketing, online sales actually increased at a rapid rate. It was at Nordstrom that the final touches were put on the "Multichannel Forensics" framework that accurately suggested that retail and online channels did not need catalog mailings to support sales growth.

In March 2007, Kevin left Nordstrom to begin his own consulting practice, called "MineThatData". Kevin utilizes his Multichannel Forensics framework to help marketers understand how customers interact with products, brands, and channels. Kevin's clients include online pure-plays, thirty million dollar catalog brands, billion dollar retail multichannel brands, and international direct marketers.

In recent months, CEOs began asking different questions, questions that focused on the long-term sales trajectory of online advertising micro-channels. Kevin expanded his Multichannel Forensics framework, resulting in what are called "Online Marketing Simulations", tools that allows CEOs, CMOs, Online Marketers, and Web Analysts to understand how online and offline customers are likely to evolve and change in the future. This information allows the online marketer to identify the "Most Valuable Path", or "MVP", the path that maps how first time buyers become loyal customers. Armed with this information, investments in keyword campaigns, affiliate marketing, and e-mail marketing change, resulting in an improved and more profitable future.

Kevin also hosts the highly popular database marketing blog, called "The MineThatData Blog", where Kevin discusses online marketing, direct marketing, database marketing, and multichannel marketing topics on a frequent basis. Kevin's Twitter following discusses key marketing issues as well.

Contact Information:

Kevin Hillstrom
President, MineThatData
E-Mail: kevinh@minethatdata.com
Website: http://minethatdata.com
Blog: http://minethatdata.com/blog
Twitter: http://twitter.com/minethatdata

Consulting Services

Kevin provides consulting services for leading online marketers and multichannel retailers. Given his experience at leading multichannel retailers like Nordstrom, Eddie Bauer, and Lands' End, Kevin brings more than two decades of unique executive and analytical experience to his projects.

There are many popular projects that Kevin performs for CEOs and CMOs.

- Online Marketing Simulations, the subject of this book, tailored to CEOs, CMOs, Online Marketing Executives, Online Marketing Directors, and Web Analytics Experts.

- Multichannel Forensics Projects, designed to determine which customers no longer need to receive catalog mailings, and outline which customers should receive a mix of e-mail marketing and catalog marketing. A typical Multichannel Forensics Project for a $75,000,000 brand results in about $250,000 to $750,000 of annual profit opportunity, well worth the average cost of a Multichannel Forensics project. A typical Multichannel Forensics or Online Marketing Simulation project takes four weeks to complete, and costs between $9,000 and $40,000, depending upon how many twelve-month buyers your business has.

- Persona and Segmentation Projects, especially useful for e-mail marketers looking to classify customers into actionable segments that can receive targeted and personalized e-mail marketing messages.

- Price Elasticity Projects, where we determine how many units of an item will sell, given different pricing strategies. You will learn which price generates the most gross margin dollars for a given item, and you will receive a spreadsheet that allows you to play with different scenarios.

- Database Marketing Audits, designed to help the CEO/CMO understand how your business stacks up against competing organizations. The typical two-day audit results in a roadmap for success, outlining database strategies and marketing strategies and staffing strategies that yield profitable outcomes.

Contact me (kevinh@minethatdata.com) for project details.

Online Marketing Simulations

Chapter 1: A Little History

In the days prior to the internet revolution, the customer received merchandise offerings in her mailbox.

Direct marketers were reasonably sophisticated, given the rudimentary state of mainframe campaign reporting systems. Direct marketers quickly learned that success wasn't based on individual mailing campaign. No, success was measured by cultivating a customer base that was likely to spend money in the future.

Direct marketers actively measured the results of "cannibalization studies". Customers were placed into A/B tests, or multivariate tests (I once created and analyzed a 2^7 factorial design. It answered a lot of questions!). Direct marketers learned that measuring the business on the basis of individual campaigns led to "confusing" results. The direct marketer might observe a situation where a campaign is added, and the new campaign does really well, but the existing campaigns mailed around the new campaign no longer performed well. Cannibalization testing proved that if the new campaign had not been added, the old campaigns would have performed to expectations.

The direct marketer learned that measuring customer behavior over time made more sense than analyzing customer performance in individual campaigns. And not surprisingly, if you needed to measure customer behavior over time, you could also predict customer behavior over time, gaining insight into what the future might hold.

In my final year at Lands' End, back in 1995, I was asked to create a tool that allowed our circulation managers to "predict the future". In other words, the circulation managers wanted to know how many customers would exist in key segments in the next two, three, four, and five years. Given this knowledge, the circulation managers would alter contact strategies, allowing them to generate the most profit possible. In essence, our circulation managers wanted to use a simulation tool to understand future customer behavior.

That was 1995, in the old-school world of direct marketing.

Fast forward to the "internet era", which essentially began in 1995.

The first thirteen years of the internet era were a lot of fun! You put a bunch of merchandise up on a website, you optimized your website for search engines, you leverage offline activities, and you sold a bunch of stuff.

You didn't need to be a genius to be successful, though being a genius clearly helped! Because customers were eager to try e-commerce, you were blessed to be in the right place at the right time. Each year, the number of customers purchasing via e-commerce increased, as e-commerce cannibalized existing channels and created demand all by itself.

Everything changed in September, 2008.

When the economy collapsed, so did easy and unfettered e-commerce growth.

It didn't take long for the tone of the projects I worked on to change. Within months, CEOs were asking very different questions. For the first time, I wasn't being asked to justify whether brands should continue to invest marketing dollars in offline channels. Instead, I was being asked to justify investment levels in online channels.

CEOs knew that e-mail marketing, pay-per-click, affiliate marketing, paid search, and all other online marketing generated sales. But fifteen years of focusing on "conversions", the act of a customer purchasing merchandise right now because of one or more marketing activities in the recent past, caused us to not thoroughly understand how online channels fit together.

CEOs wanted to understand if a customer acquired via paid search would become an e-mail subscriber.

CEOs wanted to understand if a customer acquired via affiliate marketing would become a loyal customer.

CEOs wanted to understand what would happen to customer loyalty if e-mail marketing frequency were significantly altered.

And most important, CEOs wanted to understand how the e-commerce channel would grow (or shrink) in the future. They wanted to see how everything that happens online fits together to create a positive or negative outcome.

In other words, CEOs wanted to replicate the business understanding that direct marketers were focused on in the pre-internet era.

The thought process is different. Leaders weren't asking for integrated campaigns. Leaders were asking to see how everything could fit together today in a way that fueled online sales for years to come.

This is one place where classic web analytics fail to provide business leaders the insight they need. Web analytics software packages are geared to measure the past. In no way does this text set out to criticize web analytics practitioners or online marketers. Simply put, the web analytics and online marketing practitioner was never given tools that allow them to understand the future. Maybe this text will be an inspiration to our vendor community to incorporate forward-looking views of customer behavior in their software offering.

That's what we are going to do in this text. We're going to study an e-commerce brand, and we're going to understand how customers interact with different online marketing channels and merchandise divisions. We are going to predict the sales trajectory of each online channel. We are going to see how a customer who purchased from one merchandise division differs from a customer who purchased from another merchandise division, and how that subtle difference plays a significant role in the shaping of the future.

It is the future that matters, folks.

Think about the weather forecast that you consult on a daily or weekly basis.

Now you're probably mumbling something under your breath about how meteorologists are always wrong. And they *are* always wrong! But, on average, they are reasonably accurate. When you wake up on a Wednesday morning, you have a good idea what the weather might be like during the weekend, right?

You plan your life around the weather forecast. Heck, you plan your life around a lot of things that you can predict. You know what your mortgage payment will be every month, if you have a fixed mortgage. You know what time your favorite television show is on each week. Heck, you can predict how your spouse will react to just about any situation, and plan accordingly!

So why do so few of us focus on predicting where our e-commerce business is headed? And I'm not talking about the generic forecasts produced by research organizations, predictions of twelve percent or fifteen percent industry-wide growth. I'm talking about all of us who focus on e-commerce marketing. Why don't we know where our businesses are headed?

When organic online growth runs out, we'll want to make sure that people have the tools necessary to understand what is going to happen. That's what this handbook is about. We'll spend a lot of time talking about e-commerce forecasting, about simulating where our business is headed, about understanding which customer segments provide the best long-term value.

I'll start by focusing on a very simple and generic example, so that you can see the nuts and bolts that fuel the simulation. Once we've mastered the basics, we'll move on to a much larger simulation, one with 240 customer segments. We'll look at five segments that comprise customer quality, combined with eight segments that outline the preferred advertising channel used by the customer (affiliates, e-mail, offline, print ads, social media, search, non-coded, multi-preference), combined with six merchandise divisions that the customer prefers. Five by eight by six yields 240 customer segments. I'll demonstrate how knowledge of these segments allows the marketer to make significant differences to the marketing strategy of a business, yielding outcomes that outperform the expected trajectory based on current business practices.

The purpose of this handbook is to encourage you, the CEO, CMO, Online Marketer, or Web Analytics expert, to think differently about your business. I want for you to understand how a thorough understanding of future customer behavior causes one to make very different campaign-based decisions. I want for the online community to understand that optimizing campaign performance is not the same as optimizing business performance. I want for the online community to move beyond technology and tactics. I want for the online community to become strategic leaders.

Keep these thoughts in mind as you work through the examples in this test. Please work on your own examples, not focusing solely on the exercises offered in this handbook. Train yourself to always be thinking whether your decisions influence long-term business health. And most important, have fun!! The concepts in this handbook are fundamentally different than most of the online analytics you read about.

Finally, this simulation tool is reasonably "low-tech". If you use any search engine, you will find sophisticated simulation software solutions that can model just about any business problem. Feel free to purchase these solutions, and leverage them to better understand the future. I am not advocating the specific methodology and toolset outlined in this book. I am advocating the use of tools and techniques to understand and act upon future customer behavior.

Chapter 2: A Simple Example

Let's start with a fairly easy situation to track. We'll look at a situation where an e-commerce brand grades customers, based on value. This business grades each customer, just like we were graded when we were in school.
- Grade of "A" = Best Customers.
- Grade of "B" = Good Customers.
- Grade of "C" = Average Customers.
- Grade of "D" = Marginal Customers.
- Grade of "F" = Unproductive Customers.

At the start of a year, customers fall into one of the five segments. Given the segment the customer falls into, the customer can migrate to any of the five segments next year.

For instance, let's take a look at all customers with a grade of "C", as of December 31, 2008. During 2009, a percentage of the customers will purchase again. Let's pretend that the percentage is 20%. This, of course, is a metric called the "Repurchase Rate".

Among the customers who repurchase, many migrate to "Best Customer" status. Let's look at where customers who repurchase migrate to:
- 60% earn a Grade of "A".
- 40% earn a Grade of "B".
- 0% earn grades of "C", "D", or "F",

If the customer purchases, the customer becomes more valuable to the business.

Now, let's look at the 80% of customers who do not purchase during 2009. Which segment do these customers migrate to?
- 0% earn a Grade of "A", 0% earn a Grade of "B".
- 10% maintain a Grade of "C".

17

- 50% fall to a Grade of "D".
- 40% fall to a Grade of "F".

So, we have 20% of the customers who repurchase, and 80% who do not repurchase. Within this repurchase rate activity, customers migrate across segments as illustrated above. This yields the following distribution of customers at the end of 2009:
- 12% earn a Grade of "A"
- 8% earn a Grade of "B".
- 8% maintain a Grade of "C".
- 40% fall to a Grade of "D".
- 32% fall to a Grade of "F".

If a customer repurchases, the customer will spend a certain amount of money with your brand, say $200. If we had 1,000 customers who start the year with a grade of "C", then 20% repurchase, spending $200. This segment will generate 1,000 * 0.20 * $200 = $40,000.

At this point, we have the data necessary to run a simulation of future behavior. We compile similar metrics for customers who start 2009 with grades of "A", "B", "C" (we already illustrated this example above), "D", and "F".

Here is a table that illustrates how all customers migrate during the next twelve months:

Table #1: Customer Migration

	Repurchase?	% Who Migrate	Amount Spent	Migrate To Grade = A	Migrate To Grade = B	Migrate To Grade = C	Migrate To Grade = D	Migrate To Grade = F
Customer Migration Table: Simple Five Grade Example								
Grade = A	Yes	60.0%	$300	90.0%	10.0%	0.0%	0.0%	0.0%
	No	40.0%	$0	10.0%	30.0%	30.0%	30.0%	0.0%
Grade = B	Yes	40.0%	$250	70.0%	30.0%	0.0%	0.0%	0.0%
	No	60.0%	$0	0.0%	10.0%	40.0%	30.0%	20.0%
Grade = C	Yes	20.0%	$225	60.0%	40.0%	0.0%	0.0%	0.0%
	No	80.0%	$0	0.0%	0.0%	10.0%	50.0%	40.0%
Grade = D	Yes	10.0%	$200	40.0%	50.0%	10.0%	0.0%	0.0%
	No	90.0%	$0	0.0%	0.0%	0.0%	30.0%	70.0%
Grade = F	Yes	5.0%	$175	20.0%	40.0%	30.0%	10.0%	0.0%
	No	95.0%	$0	0.0%	0.0%	0.0%	0.0%	100.0%
New Buyers	Yes	100.0%	$150	10.0%	30.0%	60.0%	0.0%	0.0%

This is the table we need, in order to complete the simulation. With this information, and a count of the number of customers who reside in each segment at the start of 2009, we can simulate where this business is headed over the course of the next five years.

By doing all of the multiplications, we arrive at the following table:

Table #2: A Five Year Simulation

	Begin	After Year 1	After Year 2	After Year 3	After Year 4	After Year 5
Customer Migration Table: Five Year Simulation						
Grade = A	12,000	13,030	13,475	13,874	14,307	14,780
Grade = B	10,000	9,290	9,471	9,760	10,086	10,432
Grade = C	11,000	11,395	11,535	11,784	12,058	12,343
Grade = D	15,000	11,865	11,234	11,255	11,506	11,837
Grade = F	35,000	47,420	57,285	66,326	75,043	83,608
Newbies		10,000	10,000	10,000	10,000	10,000
Total Spend		$5,761,250	$5,939,400	$6,117,547	$6,309,053	$6,513,253

Given the way customers migrate across different grades, we are able to simulate the future sales trajectory of this business, and we are able to simulate how many customers will achieve good, average, or marginal grades in the future.

And clearly, this is a business that is forecast to experience anemic growth.

If we want to see what might happen to the business if we change customer acquisition strategies, we simply change the number of customers in the customer acquisition segments over time. Let's see what happens if we acquire 15,000 new customers per year, instead of just 10,000 customers per year.

Table #3: 15,000 New Customers per Year

Customer Migration Table: Five Year Simulation						
	Begin	After Year 1	After Year 2	After Year 3	After Year 4	After Year 5
Grade = A	12,000	13,530	15,045	16,384	17,593	18,708
Grade = B	10,000	10,790	11,571	12,313	13,011	13,675
Grade = C	11,000	14,395	15,195	15,802	16,369	16,911
Grade = D	15,000	11,865	12,764	13,705	14,552	15,337
Grade = F	35,000	47,420	58,425	69,796	81,475	93,368
Newbies		15,000	15,000	15,000	15,000	15,000
Total Spend		$6,511,250	$7,064,400	$7,565,422	$8,026,334	$8,458,356

Now we're looking at health growth, aren't we? We can clearly see that a 50% increase in new customers results in a 16% increase in demand after just one year, and close to a 30% increase in demand after five years.

We can also see what impact an improving economy might have. Let's go back to acquiring just 10,000 new customers, per year. We will increase repurchase rates, by segment, by 15%. Take a look at the outcome of the simulation.

Table #4: A 15% Increase in Customer Retention

Customer Migration Table: Five Year Simulation

	Begin	After Year 1	After Year 2	After Year 3	After Year 4	After Year 5
Grade = A	12,000	14,655	16,183	17,405	18,511	19,559
Grade = B	10,000	9,544	9,926	10,425	10,941	11,454
Grade = C	11,000	10,899	11,198	11,585	11,972	12,351
Grade = D	15,000	11,155	10,336	10,487	10,915	11,407
Grade = F	35,000	46,748	55,358	63,099	70,661	78,229
Newbies		10,000	10,000	10,000	10,000	10,000
Total Spend		$6,400,438	$6,921,981	$7,365,510	$7,777,263	$8,171,685

Notice that when the economy improves, we see healthy sales growth!

Now we'll combine a 15% growth in retention rates with a 50% increase in new customer acquisition. Look out!!

Table #4: Increases of 15% in Retention, 50% in Acquisition

Customer Migration Table: Five Year Simulation

	Begin	After Year 1	After Year 2	After Year 3	After Year 4	After Year 5
Grade = A	12,000	15,155	17,906	20,295	22,428	24,374
Grade = B	10,000	11,044	12,071	13,055	13,983	14,861
Grade = C	11,000	13,899	14,800	15,521	16,194	16,833
Grade = D	15,000	11,155	11,780	12,771	13,750	14,677
Grade = F	35,000	46,748	56,444	66,358	76,645	87,254
Newbies		15,000	15,000	15,000	15,000	15,000
Total Spend		$7,150,438	$8,103,231	$8,949,375	$9,717,019	$10,426,234

This is a very simple example, but one that outlines how the trajectory of a business is likely to change, given the strategic changes you make to a business over time.

Simple examples like this translate well to the complexity of typical Online Marketing Simulations. Instead of focusing on just five segments, I am going to focus on a situation where a business has customers that span 240 segments. The exact same logic that yielded the outcomes in this example will drive the understanding of how a modern e-commerce business evolves and changes.

The added complexity is necessary to thoroughly understand how customers behave across a modern e-commerce business. Customers interact across a variety of what I call advertising "micro-channels".

Micro-channels represent the advertising activities that cause a customer to purchase from us. As we explore Online Marketing Simulations (OMS), we'll learn whether a paid search buyer becomes an e-mail customer, or whether a customer acquired via an affiliate marketing program becomes a loyal buyer. We will thoroughly understand how customers interact with merchandise divisions and channels. Finally, we'll have an idea of how our actions influence future customer behavior.

Are you ready to tackle the 240 segment Online Marketing Simulation?

Chapter 3: The Basics

Let's begin our study of a sample business by reviewing a downloadable spreadsheet.

http://minethatdata.com/KevinHillstromOMSBook.xlsx

This is a large file, about 10mb in size, so please give the file a moment to download.

When you open the spreadsheet, you will be greeted with a series of tables that illustrate some of the characteristics about this business. Let's review the upper-left-hand corner of the spreadsheet.

Table #5: Summary Statistics

The Online Marketing Simulation: 240 Segment Analysis

	Year 1	Year 2	Year 3	Year 4	Year 5
Change in Retention	1.00	1.00	1.00	1.00	1.00
Change in Acquisition	1.00	1.00	1.00	1.00	1.00
Change in Spend	1.00	1.00	1.00	1.00	1.00
	Year 1	Year 2	Year 3	Year 4	Year 5
Total Buyers On File	1,162,446	1,343,088	1,523,730	1,704,372	1,885,014
Total 12 Month Buyers	321,902	336,621	349,641	361,468	372,445
Total New Buyers	180,642	180,642	180,642	180,642	180,642
Total Demand	$73,781,435	$78,119,480	$81,997,142	$85,519,549	$88,767,363
Total Orders	498,760	525,341	548,952	570,335	590,051
Total Items	1,600,977	1,691,280	1,771,460	1,844,097	1,911,044
Orders per Buyer	1.549	1.561	1.570	1.578	1.584
Items per Order	3.210	3.219	3.227	3.233	3.239
Price per Item	$46.09	$46.19	$46.29	$46.37	$46.45
Average Order Value	$147.93	$148.70	$149.37	$149.95	$150.44
Demand per Buyer	$229.20	$232.07	$234.52	$236.59	$238.34
Total Customers = "A"	97,791	105,616	112,706	119,146	125,049
Total Customers = "B"	191,080	199,696	207,298	214,227	220,702
Total Customers = "C"	212,743	223,824	233,688	242,455	250,404
Total Customers = "D"	230,285	260,761	280,111	294,362	305,878
Total Customers = "F"	430,546	553,191	689,926	834,182	982,980

There is a lot of information here, so we're going to go through it carefully. Please feel free to skip ahead if you do not want to wade through the descriptions of the cells within the table.

Look at columns C - G. These columns represent the outcome of each of five simulated years. You will want to review these columns after making subtle changes to each simulated run you perform.

Take a look at Row 10 in the spreadsheet. Cells C10 - G10 illustrate how many buyers have ever purchased from this business, based on the results of the simulation.

Cells C11 - G11 are a bit more important, outlining the number of customers who purchased from this business during the past twelve months. For so many e-commerce companies, this is one of the most important metrics (or key performance indicators, known as a "KPI"). Healthy businesses tend to have an increasing number of highly productive twelve-month buyers over time.

Cells C12 - G12 illustrate the number of new customers added to the business, on an annual basis. Most business leaders eventually learn that customer acquisition is one of the most important aspects of running a profitable and growing e-commerce business.

Cells C13 - G13 show how much demand was generated by the conditions in the simulation. These five cells are the most important ones in the simulation! We get to see how our actions change the future trajectory of the business. We will return to these five cells over and over again as we work through various examples.

Cells C14 - G14 quantify how many orders were placed during each year of simulated results.

Cells C15 – G15 quantify how many items were purchased during each year of simulated results.

Cells C16 – G16 illustrate an important metric, called "Orders per Buyer". Healthy businesses tend to yield simulated results where Orders per Buyer increase every single year. This is always a row that is worth paying close attention to.

Cells C17 – G17 represent a metric called "Items per Order". We want to have a healthy business where customers order more and more items per order.

However, we have to pay close attention to how this metric interacts with another metric, in Cells C18 – G18, called "Price per Item". This set of cells illustrate how much the average customer spent per item purchased. We often see instances where customers buy more expensive items, but purchase fewer of them.

When that happens, we get to see the dynamic in cells C19 – G19, represented here as "Average Order Value". The metric measures how much a customer spent when placing an order.

We also want to pay attention to cells C20 – G20, illustrating a metric called "Demand per Buyer". Here, we take total demand (C13 – G13), and divide it by the number of twelve month buyers (C11 – G11). In theory, as a business becomes stronger, we have a customer base that spends more and more per year. The numbers in this row can be influenced by the mix of loyal buyers and new buyers in the business. For instance, if you aggressively try to acquire new customers, you'll end up with a customer base that has a disproportionate number of low spenders, in the short-term. Over time, many of the newly acquire customers will become loyal buyers, yielding a high number of high-spending customers.

Cells C21 - G21 count the number of customers graded as "A". In my simulations, I like to divide the customer base into those who are exceptional (Grade = "A"), good (Grade = "B"), average (Grade = "C"), marginal (Grade = "D"), and poor (Grade = "F"). This allows us to see how the customer file changes and migrates as we execute different marketing strategies. The goal, as always, is to migrate as many customers as possible into high-value segments. We will learn, of course, that this is a very difficult thing to do, that customer quality is in a continual state of decay.

We will return to this corner of the spreadsheet on a repeated basis, to understand how our scenarios result in changes to the business.

Now let's look at another portion of the spreadsheet, represented by cells J1 - N17.

Table #6: Demand Totals by Micro-Channel And Merchandise Division

Demand by Segmentation Indicators					
Indicator	Year 1	Year 2	Year 3	Year 4	Year 5
Affiliates	$4,012,146	$4,310,385	$4,569,031	$4,798,996	$5,007,713
Offline Ads	$19,487,111	$20,736,399	$21,864,852	$22,896,743	$23,852,158
E-Mail	$19,292,388	$20,606,188	$21,804,864	$22,897,522	$23,904,018
Soc. Media	$2,828,562	$2,887,142	$2,937,563	$2,982,381	$3,023,928
Print Ads	$4,939,471	$5,041,806	$5,126,219	$5,201,918	$5,273,012
Search	$5,578,806	$5,878,662	$6,141,188	$6,378,085	$6,595,827
No Source	$17,642,950	$18,658,898	$19,553,424	$20,363,904	$21,110,707
Merch Div 1	$12,186,889	$12,930,957	$13,590,366	$14,186,282	$14,733,781
Merch Div 2	$19,448,461	$20,270,786	$21,038,790	$21,756,723	$22,433,242
Merch Div 3	$19,873,920	$21,162,461	$22,281,524	$23,278,861	$24,186,265
Merch Div 4	$7,073,158	$7,504,048	$7,889,120	$8,238,785	$8,560,984
Merch Div 5	$15,199,006	$16,251,227	$17,197,343	$18,058,898	$18,853,091
Demand	$73,781,435	$78,119,480	$81,997,142	$85,519,549	$88,767,363
Margin	$38,904,020	$41,138,942	$43,148,331	$44,980,559	$46,673,971

This portion of the spreadsheet is calibrated to accept one hundred different forecasts. For the purpose of the example we're going to explore, I only used fourteen different micro-channels or merchandise divisions.

This business generates sales online via several different advertising micro-channels.
- Cells J4 - N4 = Affiliate Marketing.
- Cells J5 - N5 = Offline Advertising.
- Cells J6 - N6 = E-Mail Marketing.
- Cells J7 - N7 = Social Media.
- Cells J8 - N8 = Print Ads in Magazines & Newspapers.
- Cells J9 - N9 = Paid Search.
- Cells J10 - N10 = No Source.

Each column represents the predicted sales to be obtained from each micro-channel during the next five years. As we work through various examples, we'll be able to see how changes in one micro-channel (say e-mail) impact demand in another micro-channel, like paid search marketing.

Now take a look at J11 - N11, on down to J15 - N15. Each row represents the sales that will be generated within each merchandise division for this e-commerce brand. Think of merchandise divisions as being the merchandise that is sold within each tab running across the top of a website. In our example, we are going to explore how customers who purchase from different merchandise divisions have a different long-term trajectory than do other customers. We'll also see if customers who purchase from certain advertising micro-channels tend to purchase from specific merchandise divisions.

Cells J16 - N16 represents total demand. J17 - N17 represents gross margin dollars.

As mentioned earlier, there is room for up to one-hundred different segment identifiers in this simulation, I'm only choosing to analyze the fourteen micro-channels and merchandise divisions featured here. Should you decide to create your own spreadsheet, you will be able to add as many segment identifiers as you wish.

We shift our focus to cells W1 - BI51. This simulation has 240 segments. The number of customers in each segment is illustrated in this portion of the spreadsheet.

Table #7: Segment Customer Counts, Example

Customer Counts In Each Of 240 Segments: Grade = A						
Segment	Year 0	Year 1	Year 2	Year 3	Year 4	Year 5
A Aff MD1	189	203	209	215	220	224
A Aff MD2	153	144	142	143	146	149
A Aff MD3	387	441	474	499	520	539
A Aff MD4	54	62	69	75	80	84
A Aff MD5	402	438	466	489	510	529
A Aff MDM	882	982	1,059	1,123	1,179	1,228
A Off MD1	1,554	1,636	1,714	1,791	1,867	1,942
A Off MD2	2,343	2,309	2,352	2,426	2,512	2,603
A Off MD3	2,445	2,662	2,837	2,981	3,105	3,215
A Off MD4	369	354	364	381	400	420
A Off MD5	2,160	2,225	2,332	2,447	2,558	2,664
A OFF MDM	9,786	10,419	11,138	11,868	12,571	13,239
A EM MD1	1,734	1,866	1,978	2,074	2,156	2,229
A EM MD2	2,961	2,669	2,631	2,679	2,754	2,839
A EM MD3	2,883	3,179	3,432	3,641	3,815	3,964
A EM MD4	387	410	430	448	463	476
A EM MD5	3,117	3,214	3,379	3,553	3,724	3,888
A EM MDM	11,187	11,971	12,867	13,773	14,647	15,474

Each segment has three different abbreviations.

Abbreviation #1 = Customer Quality (A, B, C, D, or F). There are five grades. A grade of "A" is good, a grade of "F" is not so good!

Abbreviation #2 = Advertising Micro-Channel (Affiliates, Offline Ads, E-Mail, Social Media, Print Ads, Search, No Source, Multiple Micro-Channels). The abbreviations are

AFF, OFF, EM, SM, PA, SR, NS, ML. There are eight micro-channel combinations.

Abbreviation #3 = Merchandise Division (Merchandise Division #1, Merchandise Division #2, Merchandise Division #3, Merchandise Division #4, Merchandise Division #5, Multiple Merchandise Divisions). The abbreviations are MD1, MD2, MD3, MD4, MD5, MDM. There are six merchandise division combinations.

Each of the 240 segments represent a combination of customer quality, micro-channel preference, and merchandise division preference.

- A EM MDM = Customer Grade = A, Prefers E-Mail Marketing, and Buys from Multiple Merchandise Divisions.

For the purpose of this analysis, any customer who spent at least 55% of their dollars in an advertising micro-channel or merchandise division is then assigned to that micro-channel or merchandise division. If a customer splits money across advertising micro-channels or merchandise divisions, then the customer is classified as "multiple".

Honestly, there is no right or wrong way to do this. I am simply using this structure so that the examples can be easily understood, as we work our way through this handbook.

In fact, when I work on OMS projects for clients, I go with a framework that is considerably more complex. I use a Factor Analysis to reduce the dimensionality of advertising micro-channels, merchandise divisions, price points, discounts and promotions, and website click-stream data. I create 48 unique segments, based on unique combinations, and then multiply the five customer grades by forty-eight unique segments to get to 240 total customer segments. This methodology is more difficult for somebody to understand, but it does yield more interesting results!

This concludes the reporting portion of the spreadsheet. Let's review where some of the key customer data elements are added to the spreadsheet.

Please page down to cells A99 – D580.

The red numbers represent existing housefile customer counts, by segment. Cell B101 says we are beginning the simulation with 189 customers in segment "A Aff MD1" (Grade = A, Preference = Affiliate Marketing, Preference = Merchandise Division #1).

The light blue numbers represent the probability of a customer in that segment repurchasing in the next twelve months. Cell C101 has the value of 0.4800. This means that customers in segment "A Aff MD1" have a 48% chance of purchasing again in the next twelve months. Notice that, as you page down the spreadsheet, the percentages decrease as we get to customers with a Grade = B, Grade = C, Grade = D, and Grade = F. In fact, by the time we get to the "Fs", we notice that the likelihood of a customer purchasing again is very low.

This is the place in the spreadsheet where we enter the customer counts that begin the simulation. Columns F – AJ show how many customers, by year, are going to purchase or not purchase. These columns fuel the remainder of the simulation.

Page down to cell B341. Notice that the color of the cells change to green. These are the segment counts for new-to-file customers, customers that will be acquired in each of the next five years in each segment.

I spent a lot of time talking about column B. You will see the same file counts in column D. As you make changes to the spreadsheet, you are likely to forget what the beginning inventory of customers are. Just copy the counts in column

D and paste them in column B if you need to refresh t spreadsheet.

Page down to cell A1500. In this portion of the spreadsheet, I do not name segments as mentioned above, instead, I use a numerical designation ... segments 1-240, customer acquisition segments are assigned the same segment number, plus a value of 300, meaning new customers into segment one are assigned to segment 301.

Cells A1500 - ML2382 represent the raw data that I obtained, using computer programming (SPSS) against a customer file that has one row for every item a customer purchased. Let's review some of the columns, so that you know what data is outlined here.

Column B tells us if the customer segment repurchased or not. A value of "1" equals repurchase, a value of "0" represents the fact that the customer did not repurchase.

Columns D - IJ tell us the percentage of customers who migrate to future segments (numbered 1 - 240).

Column IM illustrates how much demand this customer segment will spend.

Column IN tells us how many orders the customer segment will place.

Column IO outlines how many items the customer will purchase.

Columns IP - MK illustrate how much will be spent in each of the advertising micro-channels or merchandise divisions outlined in the top portion of the spreadsheet.

Cells A1500 - ML2382 provide the raw data that fuels the entire spreadsheet. Next, page down to cell A2501.

Cells A2501 - MK3222 represent the calculations for the first year of the simulation. Once the simulation has been completed for the first year, key cells at the top of the spreadsheet are populated accordingly. Once populated, we are ready to run the simulation for the second year.

Cells A3501 - MK4222 represent year two of the simulation.

Cells A4501 - MK5222 represent year three of the simulation.

Cells A5501 - MK6222 represent year four of the simulation.

Cells A6501 - MK7222 represent year five of the simulation.

That's the simulation, folks! You populate the appropriate cells with customer performance data, and then you can run many different scenarios that outline where your business is headed over the next five years!

At the end of this book, you will get to see fifty or sixty pages of programming code that populate the spreadsheet. This is the type of work I do for my clients. You may have a technical person on staff who can do this for you. You may ask me to do this for you. Or you may go with a much simpler simulation strategy (like the one outlined at the start of this book).

The Purple Cells: C5 - G7

At the very top of the spreadsheet, you will notice a series of cells with purple text. These are global scalars that allow you to see what happens, at a high level, if you change various assumptions.

Cells C5 - G5 allow you to change customer retention assumptions. If you enter the value 1.10 into each of these cells, you are assuming that customer retention rates will be improved by ten percent. If you enter the value 0.90 into each of these cells, you are assuming that customer retention rates will be decreased by ten percent.

Cells C6 – G6 allow you to change customer acquisition assumptions. If you enter the value 1.20 into each of these cells, you are assuming that customer acquisition counts will be improved by twenty percent. If you enter the value 0.80 into each of these cells, you are assuming that customer acquisition counts will be decreased by twenty percent.

Cells C7 – G7 allow you to change spending assumptions. If you enter the value 1.30 into each of these cells, you are assuming that customers will spend thirty percent more, per transaction, than is currently assumed. If you enter the value 0.70 into each of these cells, you are assuming that customers will spend thirty percent less, per transaction, than is currently assumed.

Most of the time, I use these cells to get a thorough understanding of what it will take to move the business in the direction that the CEO wants to move the business.

Chapter 4: Changes in Global Assumptions

Let's look at what happens to our simulation when we change global assumptions.

Recall our base case, illustrated below:

Table #8: Our Base Case

The Online Marketing Simulation: 240 Segment Analysis					
	Year 1	Year 2	Year 3	Year 4	Year 5
Change in Retention	1.00	1.00	1.00	1.00	1.00
Change in Acquisition	1.00	1.00	1.00	1.00	1.00
Change in Spend	1.00	1.00	1.00	1.00	1.00
	Year 1	Year 2	Year 3	Year 4	Year 5
Total Buyers On File	1,162,446	1,343,088	1,523,730	1,704,372	1,885,014
Total 12 Month Buyers	321,902	336,621	349,641	361,468	372,445
Total New Buyers	180,642	180,642	180,642	180,642	180,642
Total Demand	$73,781,435	$78,119,480	$81,997,142	$85,519,549	$88,767,363
Total Orders	498,760	525,341	548,952	570,335	590,051
Total Items	1,600,977	1,691,280	1,771,460	1,844,097	1,911,044
Orders per Buyer	1.549	1.561	1.570	1.578	1.584
Items per Order	3.210	3.219	3.227	3.233	3.239
Price per Item	$46.09	$46.19	$46.29	$46.37	$46.45
Average Order Value	$147.93	$148.70	$149.37	$149.95	$150.44
Demand per Buyer	$229.20	$232.07	$234.52	$236.59	$238.34
Total Customers = "A"	97,791	105,616	112,706	119,146	125,049
Total Customers = "B"	191,080	199,696	207,298	214,227	220,702
Total Customers = "C"	212,743	223,824	233,688	242,455	250,404
Total Customers = "D"	230,285	260,761	280,111	294,362	305,878
Total Customers = "F"	430,546	553,191	689,926	834,182	982,980

In this base case, demand is expected to grow over the next five years.
- $73.8 million in Year 1.
- $78.1 million in Year 2.
- $82.0 million in Year 3.
- $85.5 million in Year 4.
- $88.8 million in Year 5.

Now let's try something simple. Let's make the assumption that next year, you find something magical, something that allows you for just one year to improve customer retention by ten percent. In cell C5, enter the number 1.10. Let's see what this does to the future of the business.

Table #9: Year 1 Retention Improves By 10%

The Online Marketing Simulation: 240 Segment Analysis					
	Year 1	Year 2	Year 3	Year 4	Year 5
Change in Retention	1.10	1.00	1.00	1.00	1.00
Change in Acquisition	1.00	1.00	1.00	1.00	1.00
Change in Spend	1.00	1.00	1.00	1.00	1.00
	Year 1	Year 2	Year 3	Year 4	Year 5
Total Buyers On File	1,162,446	1,343,088	1,523,730	1,704,372	1,885,014
Total 12 Month Buyers	336,028	340,376	352,220	363,393	373,918
Total New Buyers	180,642	180,642	180,642	180,642	180,642
Total Demand	$78,040,083	$79,745,628	$83,025,961	$86,249,527	$89,312,750
Total Orders	524,526	534,568	554,861	574,553	593,210
Total Items	1,688,401	1,723,704	1,792,114	1,858,825	1,922,076
Orders per Buyer	1.561	1.571	1.575	1.581	1.586
Items per Order	3.219	3.224	3.230	3.235	3.240
Price per Item	$46.22	$46.26	$46.33	$46.40	$46.47
Average Order Value	$148.78	$149.18	$149.63	$150.12	$150.56
Demand per Buyer	$232.24	$234.29	$235.72	$237.34	$238.86
Total Customers = "A"	104,379	109,134	114,945	120,722	126,222
Total Customers = "B"	195,502	201,403	208,497	215,142	221,410
Total Customers = "C"	206,253	226,629	235,762	244,115	251,715
Total Customers = "D"	227,122	255,834	280,312	295,608	307,289
Total Customers = "F"	429,190	550,088	684,214	828,785	978,378

Ok folks, what do you observe? Well, there's a lot of interesting things going on, right?

Look at the total number of twelve month buyers. Buyers increase by 15,000 in year one. We expect this to happen, because we'll have ten percent more existing customers, and we add the same number of new customers, yielding an increase in the number of twelve-month buyers.

Total demand increases as well, from $73.8 million to $78.0 million. This isn't hard to understand, of course. If customer loyalty is improved, we'll generate more demand.

Notice that orders per buyer exhibit an increase. When we increase retention rates, we obtain customers that are more loyal, yielding more orders per buyer. There is also a very slight increase in items per order and price per item. These are good things!! Average order value is slightly greater, as is demand per buyer.

Now take a look at the customer grades. When we increase customer retention, we migrate more customers into the best customer segments, those with a Grade = A, from 98,000 to 104,000. There are also more customers with a Grade = B. As a consequence, there are fewer customers with Grade = C, Grade = D, and Grade = F.

The consequences of a ten percent improvement in customer retention rates are apparent.

What is not apparent, however, is the downstream impact of a short-term improvement in one metric.

Remember, we did not change customer retention rates for the following four years. And yet, the simulation shows that there is a residual benefit associated with improvements in customer retention next year.

Just take a look at total five year demand, comparing the base case to the case where we improve customer retention by 10%.
- Year 1: Base = $73.8 million. Adjusted = $78.0 million.
- Year 2: Base = $78.1 million. Adjusted = $79.7 million.
- Year 3: Base = $82.0 million. Adjusted = $83.0 million.

- Year 4: Base = $85.5 million. Adjusted = $86.2 million.
- Year 5: Base = $88.8 million. Adjusted = $89.3 million.

This is fun! We fully expect the $4.7 million dollar increase generated by a 10% improvement in customer retention in year one. But we might not expect the $1.6 million dollar increase in year two, or the $1.0 million dollar increase in year three, or the $0.7 million dollar increase in year four, or the $0.5 million dollar increase in year five.

Do you understand the implications of this finding?

This means that you, as an online marketer, are taking actions today that have long-term consequences. What you do today yields a specific type of customer, a customer that exhibits different future behavior. In this case, we increase customer loyalty, and by doing so, we migrate more customers into Grade = A, and Grade = B, and those customers continue to pay back at a greater rate in future years.

It is very hard to see how this phenomenon happens when you exclusively use web analytics software to measure conversion rates at a specific point in time. This is why we need to use Online Marketing Simulations, or "OMS" as I like to call them. The OMS framework allows us to learn things about our customer base, things that are simply do not present themselves when using traditional web analytics software.

Well, if a one year improvement in retention is good, a five year improvement in retention must be really good, right?

This time, go to cells C5 - G5, and type the value 1.10 in each cell. The result is in the following table:

Table #10: A Five Year Improvement in Retention

The Online Marketing Simulation: 240 Segment Analysis					
	Year 1	Year 2	Year 3	Year 4	Year 5
Change in Retention	1.10	1.10	1.10	1.10	1.10
Change in Acquisition	1.00	1.00	1.00	1.00	1.00
Change in Spend	1.00	1.00	1.00	1.00	1.00
	Year 1	Year 2	Year 3	Year 4	Year 5
Total Buyers On File	1,162,446	1,343,088	1,523,730	1,704,372	1,885,014
Total 12 Month Buyers	336,028	356,350	374,049	390,020	404,741
Total New Buyers	180,642	180,642	180,642	180,642	180,642
Total Demand	$78,040,083	$84,600,695	$90,241,828	$95,283,905	$99,886,768
Total Orders	524,526	563,915	597,773	628,016	655,645
Total Items	1,688,401	1,823,401	1,939,196	2,042,603	2,137,019
Orders per Buyer	1.561	1.582	1.598	1.610	1.620
Items per Order	3.219	3.233	3.244	3.252	3.259
Price per Item	$46.22	$46.40	$46.54	$46.65	$46.74
Average Order Value	$148.78	$150.02	$150.96	$151.72	$152.35
Demand per Buyer	$232.24	$237.41	$241.26	$244.31	$246.79
Total Customers = "A"	104,379	116,641	127,245	136,689	145,258
Total Customers = "B"	195,502	206,227	215,607	224,142	232,089
Total Customers = "C"	206,253	219,406	230,973	241,302	250,683
Total Customers = "D"	227,122	252,407	271,248	286,161	298,710
Total Customers = "F"	429,190	548,408	678,658	816,077	958,274

Wow! Look at how the business evolves over time.
- Year 1: Base = $73.8 million. Adjusted = $78.0 million.
- Year 2: Base = $78.1 million. Adjusted = $84.6 million.
- Year 3: Base = $82.0 million. Adjusted = $90.2 million.
- Year 4: Base = $85.5 million. Adjusted = $95.3 million.
- Year 5: Base = $88.8 million. Adjusted = $99.9 million.

A consistent improvement in annual retention rates yields an impact that is similar to compound interest! A 5.7% increase after one year becomes a 12.5% increase after five years.

This is such an important finding. Nearly everything we do focuses on "campaigns", events that cause an improvement in customer performance at a point in time. This is not necessarily a bad thing. Earlier, we demonstrated that sustained improvement for one year yielded "residual" impacts that helped increase sales over time. Now, we are able to see that sustained improvement acts as a form of compound interest!

Of course, if we knew how to improve business results by 10% per year, every year, we'd already be doing that, right? This is the problem with customer loyalty. It is extremely hard to encourage customers to "become more loyal". I mean, what could McDonalds possibly do to cause you to spend 30% more money with them, per year, every single year? It isn't easy to increase loyalty.

It is, however, much easier to find new customers. Sure, it might cost a lot of money to find new customers, but that is beside the point. For most companies, if marketing is reasonably optimized for existing customers, growth happens by careful management of customer acquisition activities.

Let's look at an example. In cell C6, enter the value 0.50. This means we are going to reduce customer acquisition activities to half of current levels, for just one year.

What impact do you think this will have on this business?

Table #11: A 50% Reduction in Customer Acquisition Activities for One Year

The Online Marketing Simulation: 240 Segment Analysis					
	Year 1	Year 2	Year 3	Year 4	Year 5
Change in Retention	1.00	1.00	1.00	1.00	1.00
Change in Acquisition	0.50	1.00	1.00	1.00	1.00
Change in Spend	1.00	1.00	1.00	1.00	1.00
	Year 1	Year 2	Year 3	Year 4	Year 5
Total Buyers On File	1,072,125	1,252,767	1,433,409	1,614,051	1,794,693
Total 12 Month Buyers	231,581	315,577	334,146	349,260	362,481
Total New Buyers	90,321	180,642	180,642	180,642	180,642
Total Demand	$58,183,958	$72,174,647	$77,411,025	$81,797,312	$85,677,701
Total Orders	378,210	488,105	521,024	547,907	571,539
Total Items	1,237,611	1,567,153	1,676,884	1,767,708	1,847,783
Orders per Buyer	1.633	1.547	1.559	1.569	1.577
Items per Order	3.272	3.211	3.218	3.226	3.233
Price per Item	$47.01	$46.05	$46.16	$46.27	$46.37
Average Order Value	$153.84	$147.87	$148.57	$149.29	$149.91
Demand per Buyer	$251.25	$228.71	$231.67	$234.20	$236.36
Total Customers = "A"	87,353	95,938	104,505	112,237	119,207
Total Customers = "B"	136,240	187,063	198,290	207,264	215,077
Total Customers = "C"	187,701	183,604	219,932	232,364	242,306
Total Customers = "D"	230,285	232,970	237,046	269,050	289,730
Total Customers = "F"	430,546	553,191	673,635	793,137	928,373

Let's compare this outcome to our base case:
- Year 1: Base = $73.8 million. Adjusted = $58.2 million.
- Year 2: Base = $78.1 million. Adjusted = $72.2 million.
- Year 3: Base = $82.0 million. Adjusted = $77.4 million.
- Year 4: Base = $85.5 million. Adjusted = $81.8 million.
- Year 5: Base = $88.8 million. Adjusted = $85.7 million.

One of the fascinating outcomes of a recession is the pullback in marketing spend. Brands continually cut back on marketing expenses when business is bad, hoping to make the profit and loss statement work better. In the short-term, this can certainly work, and it often works well. But in the long-term, the results are problematic. In our example, demand is trimmed by more than fifteen million by cutting back on customer acquisition activities. However, when we bump customer acquisition spend back up to prior levels, the business does not rebound, from a top-line standpoint, as fast as we'd like for it to.

In other words, the customers we acquire at one point in time pay us back over a long period of time. Cutting customer acquisition activities in the short-term results in fewer good customers to fuel the business in the future.

Let's try an experiment. Let's see what happens if we eliminate customer acquisition altogether! Type the value "0.00" into cells C6 – G6.

Table #12: No Customer Acquisition

The Online Marketing Simulation: 240 Segment Analysis					
	Year 1	Year 2	Year 3	Year 4	Year 5
Change in Retention	1.00	1.00	1.00	1.00	1.00
Change in Acquisition	0.00	0.00	0.00	0.00	0.00
Change in Spend	1.00	1.00	1.00	1.00	1.00
	Year 1	Year 2	Year 3	Year 4	Year 5
Total Buyers On File	981,804	981,804	981,804	981,804	981,804
Total 12 Month Buyers	141,260	113,892	95,923	83,334	74,383
Total New Buyers	0	0	0	0	0
Total Demand	$42,586,480	$35,034,859	$29,740,287	$25,818,221	$22,886,711
Total Orders	257,659	209,769	177,525	154,053	136,745
Total Items	874,245	716,293	607,322	527,182	467,606
Orders per Buyer	1.824	1.842	1.851	1.849	1.838
Items per Order	3.393	3.415	3.421	3.422	3.420
Price per Item	$48.71	$48.91	$48.97	$48.97	$48.94
Average Order Value	$165.28	$167.02	$167.53	$167.59	$167.37
Demand per Buyer	$301.48	$307.61	$310.04	$309.82	$307.69
Total Customers = "A"	76,914	65,383	56,070	48,692	42,911
Total Customers = "B"	81,400	64,750	54,336	47,339	42,565
Total Customers = "C"	162,658	93,299	75,651	64,235	55,987
Total Customers = "D"	230,285	205,180	138,401	102,028	81,247
Total Customers = "F"	430,546	553,191	657,345	719,511	759,095

Oh my goodness! The business simply collapses, doesn't it? Let's compare total demand against our base case.

- Year 1: Base = $73.8 million. Adjusted = $42.6 million.
- Year 2: Base = $78.1 million. Adjusted = $35.0 million.
- Year 3: Base = $82.0 million. Adjusted = $29.7 million.
- Year 4: Base = $85.5 million. Adjusted = $25.8 million.
- Year 5: Base = $88.8 million. Adjusted = $22.9 million.

Honestly, there is nothing more important to a business than a well-executed and cost-effective customer acquisition program. Customer acquisition is the oxygen that keeps a business moving forward. 99.999% of our businesses do not employ the Wal-Mart or Starbucks or McDonalds business model, businesses that have customers who shop every week (or day). We manage businesses where we are lucky to have 40% of last year's customers come back and buy again, and we are lucky to have a customer purchase two or three times per year.

In situations where customers exhibit what I call "normal" behavior, customer acquisition is truly the oxygen that keeps a business alive.

Let's do one more experiment. Make sure cells C5 – G5, and cells C6 – G6 are populated with the value "1.00". Now, go to C7 – G7, and enter the value "1.10". This means that we are going to assume that every customer will buy items that are 10% more expensive, for the next five years --- all other dynamics are the same.

Table #13: Increase Spend Levels By 10%

The Online Marketing Simulation: 240 Segment Analysis					
	Year 1	Year 2	Year 3	Year 4	Year 5
Change in Retention	1.00	1.00	1.00	1.00	1.00
Change in Acquisition	1.00	1.00	1.00	1.00	1.00
Change in Spend	1.10	1.10	1.10	1.10	1.10
	Year 1	Year 2	Year 3	Year 4	Year 5
Total Buyers On File	1,162,446	1,343,088	1,523,730	1,704,372	1,885,014
Total 12 Month Buyers	321,902	336,621	349,641	361,468	372,445
Total New Buyers	180,642	180,642	180,642	180,642	180,642
Total Demand	$81,159,578	$85,931,428	$90,196,856	$94,071,504	$97,644,099
Total Orders	498,760	525,341	548,952	570,335	590,051
Total Items	1,600,977	1,691,280	1,771,460	1,844,097	1,911,044
Orders per Buyer	1.549	1.561	1.570	1.578	1.584
Items per Order	3.210	3.219	3.227	3.233	3.239
Price per Item	$50.69	$50.81	$50.92	$51.01	$51.09
Average Order Value	$162.72	$163.57	$164.31	$164.94	$165.48
Demand per Buyer	$252.13	$255.28	$257.97	$260.25	$262.17
Total Customers = "A"	97,791	105,616	112,706	119,146	125,049
Total Customers = "B"	191,080	199,696	207,298	214,227	220,702
Total Customers = "C"	212,743	223,824	233,688	242,455	250,404
Total Customers = "D"	230,285	260,761	280,111	294,362	305,878
Total Customers = "F"	430,546	553,191	689,926	834,182	982,980

Let's compare this outcome with the situation where customer loyalty is increased by 10%. When we increased customer retention by 10%, we ended up with a $99.9 million dollar business in year five. Here, we end up with a $97.6 million dollar business in year five.

In no way am I saying that we shouldn't encourage cross-sell or up-sell programs, programs that facilitate a greater spend per transaction than would normally be expected.

But I am going to offer you a thesis. For most "normal" e-commerce businesses, there is a hierarchy that, if followed, yields the best long-term results.

1. A robust and cost-effective customer acquisition program.
2. Merchandising strategies coupled with marketing programs that increase customer retention rates over time.
3. Cross-Sell and Up-Sell programs that increase spend per transaction.

On average, you will consistently find that the long-term payback is greatest when an e-commerce business is managed in this rank-order priority.

Chapter 5: Constant Decay

Let's take a moment, and study how customers truly evolve.

Make sure cells C5 – G5 have the value "1.00".

Make sure cells C6 – G6 have the value "0.00".

Make sure cells C7 – G7 have the value "1.00".

Please type the value "0.00" into cells B149 – B340.

What we've done here is to make sure that no new customers are added to the simulation. In addition, we are simulating what happens when we only have customers who start the simulation period with a Grade = A.

In other words, we are going to learn what happens to a cohort of customers who are at the highest level of loyalty within the business in this simulation. What do you think is going to happen? Will these customers maintain their loyalty over time, or will the customers eventually decrease in total value to the business?

Let's see what happens!

Table #14: Five Year Demand Trend for Grade = A Customers

The Online Marketing Simulation: 240 Segment Analysis					
	Year 1	Year 2	Year 3	Year 4	Year 5
Change in Retention	1.00	1.00	1.00	1.00	1.00
Change in Acquisition	0.00	0.00	0.00	0.00	0.00
Change in Spend	1.10	1.10	1.10	1.10	1.10
	Year 1	Year 2	Year 3	Year 4	Year 5
Total Buyers On File	89,211	89,211	89,211	89,211	89,211
Total 12 Month Buyers	50,626	36,865	28,611	23,033	18,977
Total New Buyers	0	0	0	0	0
Total Demand	$23,627,076	$15,502,002	$11,427,973	$8,932,963	$7,215,547
Total Orders	120,180	81,178	60,367	47,390	38,398
Total Items	427,167	283,634	210,079	164,644	133,211
Orders per Buyer	2.374	2.202	2.110	2.057	2.023
Items per Order	3.554	3.494	3.480	3.474	3.469
Price per Item	$55.31	$54.65	$54.40	$54.26	$54.17
Average Order Value	$196.60	$190.96	$189.31	$188.50	$187.91
Demand per Buyer	$466.70	$420.51	$399.42	$387.84	$380.22
Total Customers = "A"	45,850	29,853	21,805	16,890	13,527
Total Customers = "B"	22,515	17,926	14,282	11,700	9,785
Total Customers = "C"	20,846	27,066	23,470	19,299	15,805
Total Customers = "D"	0	14,366	21,880	22,371	20,308
Total Customers = "F"	0	0	7,773	18,951	29,786

In this example, customers are in a state of constant decay. We have 89,211 customers who start the simulation with a Grade = A. These customers decay over time, generating less and less demand. Take a look at the number of customers with grades of "A", "B", "C", "D", and "F". Over time, customers who start with a grade of "A" slowly erode in value. By the end of year five, only 9,785 of the original 89,211 customers have a grade of "A".

Our businesses are in a constant state of decay. Customers achieve the loftiest of heights, and then begin an inevitable period of decline.

One might intuitively think, "well, if the best customers decline, then the most marginal customers will improve, offsetting the declines among the best customers".

Let's take a look at an example, where we watch the migration of customers with a grade of "F". Re-open the spreadsheet, and perform the following steps:

Make sure cells C5 - G5 have the value "1.00".

Make sure cells C6 - G6 have the value "0.00".

Make sure cells C7 - G7 have the value "1.00".

Please type the value "0.00" into cells B149 - B340.

Table #15: Five Year Demand Trend for Grade = F Customers

The Online Marketing Simulation: 240 Segment Analysis					
	Year 1	Year 2	Year 3	Year 4	Year 5
Change in Retention	1.00	1.00	1.00	1.00	1.00
Change in Acquisition	0.00	0.00	0.00	0.00	0.00
Change in Spend	1.10	1.10	1.10	1.10	1.10
	Year 1	Year 2	Year 3	Year 4	Year 5
Total Buyers On File	326,364	326,364	326,364	326,364	326,364
Total 12 Month Buyers	6,146	7,978	9,294	10,295	11,059
Total New Buyers	0	0	0	0	0
Total Demand	$1,400,196	$2,030,814	$2,513,115	$2,887,882	$3,179,610
Total Orders	8,280	11,718	14,277	16,261	17,804
Total Items	26,720	38,356	47,196	54,082	59,450
Orders per Buyer	1.347	1.469	1.536	1.580	1.610
Items per Order	3.227	3.273	3.306	3.326	3.339
Price per Item	$52.40	$52.95	$53.25	$53.40	$53.48
Average Order Value	$169.10	$173.31	$176.03	$177.60	$178.59
Demand per Buyer	$227.82	$254.54	$270.40	$280.53	$287.51
Total Customers = "A"	1,168	2,264	3,149	3,851	4,405
Total Customers = "B"	4,516	5,570	6,260	6,775	7,163
Total Customers = "C"	462	3,582	4,996	5,935	6,631
Total Customers = "D"	0	741	3,207	5,004	6,261
Total Customers = "F"	320,218	314,207	308,751	304,799	301,904

To some extent, very marginal customers experience small improvements in customer loyalty. Over time, only 4,405 of the 326,364 customers actually achieve a grade of "A".

But the small improvement in customer loyalty among these customers never offsets the dramatic loss in customer value experienced by the very best customers, customers with a grade of "A".

I took us through this little detour to remind everybody of the importance of finding new customers. There's really nothing more important than finding new customers that have good long-term value. If we can find ways to keep customers (again, if it were easy to keep customers, we'd all be doing it, and all of our businesses would be thriving), then we need to pursue those strategies, because customer retention is like compound interest. That being said, it is far, far easier to find new customers.

The next section deals with measuring the long-term value and evolution of customers we acquire via various advertising micro-channels. We'll see how customers migrate across advertising micro-channels. We'll see how acquiring customers via certain products makes a lot more sense than acquiring customers via other products. We'll learn why a focus on efficient customer acquisition leads us to a business model with more valuable customers, making every employee within the company more successful!

Chapter 6: The Details via Micro-Channels

It is time to go into the nitty-gritty details that make Online Marketing Simulations so useful.

We're going to analyze how customers who are acquired via specific micro-channels evolve and change over time. We are going to learn how some micro-channels yield high-value customers, while other micro-channels yield customers that take advantage of a point-in-time transaction, then move on to shopping from other brands.

Let's begin our study by re-opening the simulation spreadsheet. Make sure cells C5 - G5, and C7 - G7 all have the value of "1.00".

This is important. Make sure cell C6 = "1.00". Make sure cells D6, E6, F6, and G6 have the value "0.00". This means we are only going to track customers acquired in year one, and that we won't add new customers after year one.

Next, copy all of the values in cells B101 - B580, and paste them in cells D101 - D580. I want for you to be able to go back to original counts at any time in the future, if you need to.

Ok, now I want for you to enter the value "0.00" in cells B101 - B340. We are going to work through examples of new customers, so we don't need to have any existing customers at the start of the simulation.

Now, please enter "0.00" in cells B341 - B580. This means that we have a simulation with no customers at all! This is our starting point.

All of the upcoming simulations will result in the analysis of future value of customers acquired from various advertising micro-channels. In no way am I generalizing that what I outline here will translate to your business. In other words, when a customer is acquired via search, I will outline how the customer evolves within this business. However, this does not mean that the customer will evolve in this manner in your business. The goal here is to provide examples that allow you to think about how customers behave in your business. Every business has unique dynamics that make life more interesting! Use Online Marketing Simulations to explore how your customers migrate and change over time.

In our first simulation, we're going to analyze what happens when we acquire customers via Affiliate marketing.

Affiliate Marketing

Copy the values from D341 – D346, D389 – D394, and D437 – D442 into B341 – B346, B389 – B394, and B437 – B442. All new customers come from segments with grades of "A", "B", and "C" (that's the case in this spreadsheet, your mileage will vary), so we don't have to worry about "D" and "F" customers for customer acquisition examples.

Now that you've entered the appropriate data, let's see what happens to customers acquired via affiliate marketing.

Table #16: Customers Acquired via Affiliate Marketing

The Online Marketing Simulation: 240 Segment Analysis					
	Year 1	Year 2	Year 3	Year 4	Year 5
Change in Retention	1.00	1.00	1.00	1.00	1.00
Change in Acquisition	1.00	0.00	0.00	0.00	0.00
Change in Spend	1.00	1.00	1.00	1.00	1.00
	Year 1	Year 2	Year 3	Year 4	Year 5
Total Buyers On File	6,750	6,750	6,750	6,750	6,750
Total 12 Month Buyers	6,750	1,579	989	711	551
Total New Buyers	6,750	0	0	0	0
Total Demand	$1,323,308	$468,429	$298,176	$217,458	$171,154
Total Orders	9,003	2,814	1,779	1,297	1,020
Total Items	28,068	9,700	6,078	4,371	3,433
Orders per Buyer	1.334	1.783	1.798	1.825	1.850
Items per Order	3.118	3.446	3.417	3.371	3.366
Price per Item	$47.15	$48.29	$49.06	$49.74	$49.85
Average Order Value	$146.99	$166.44	$167.64	$167.67	$167.79
Demand per Buyer	$196.05	$296.70	$301.41	$306.00	$310.47
Total Customers = "A"	834	668	488	395	325
Total Customers = "B"	4,428	966	595	408	310
Total Customers = "C"	1,488	3,067	1,023	646	477
Total Customers = "D"	0	2,049	3,226	1,698	976
Total Customers = "F"	0	0	1,418	3,603	4,663

Overall, we get to see how these customers evolve and change. The results are interesting, aren't they?

In the four years after the customer is acquired, the 6,750 affiliate marketing customers spend $1,115,218 (the sum of cells D13 - G13), for an average of $171.14 future value.

You can clearly see how these customers are in a state of constant decline. By the end of year five, only 325 of the 6,750 customers have a grade of "A".

We can also calculate a "retention rate", by dividing the number of year two buyers (1,579) by the total universe (6,750). We only keep 23% of the buyers in year two.

51

Next, we're going to look at how demand is allocated across advertising micro-channels and merchandising divisions, over time.

Table #17: Affiliate Customer Demand Trends

Demand by Segmentation Indicators					
Indicator	Year 1	Year 2	Year 3	Year 4	Year 5
Affiliates	$1,205,977	$161,248	$68,152	$37,648	$23,104
Offline Ads	$21,157	$90,485	$69,803	$56,383	$47,991
E-Mail	$24,978	$72,910	$62,539	$53,031	$45,619
Soc. Media	$8,781	$4,114	$3,073	$2,300	$1,878
Print Ads	$8,837	$2,993	$3,823	$3,091	$2,302
Search	$7,119	$28,859	$17,904	$12,855	$10,565
No Source	$46,458	$107,820	$72,883	$52,151	$39,696
Merch Div 1	$254,767	$93,703	$55,934	$38,416	$29,666
Merch Div 2	$203,819	$72,241	$55,052	$39,431	$31,367
Merch Div 3	$401,778	$131,594	$82,253	$59,972	$47,448
Merch Div 4	$116,013	$40,801	$25,938	$19,071	$15,774
Merch Div 5	$346,930	$130,090	$78,999	$60,569	$46,899
Demand	$1,323,308	$468,429	$298,176	$217,458	$171,154
Margin	$627,401	$225,180	$148,665	$109,624	$87,526

The customer acquired via affiliate marketing does not stay loyal to affiliate marketing. In fact, pay close attention to what happens as you approach year five. The affiliate marketing customer switches loyalty to generic website orders (no source), offline ads, and e-mail marketing.

Also pay attention to search. One of the mysteries of e-commerce is in search marketing. Every customer that is acquired will, to some extent, use search marketing in the future to make purchase decisions. This means that every new customer has a built-in future cost that needs to be accounted for. You acquire a customer from any source, and then Google starts counting future dollars.

Allow me to say that again. You acquire a customer from any source (online or offline), and then Google starts counting future dollars!

Also notice that the affiliate marketing customer has a clear preference for merchandise from merchandise division #3 and merchandise division #5. We will compare the affiliate marketing customer against other advertising micro-channels, to understand how merchandise preferences influence future value.

Offline Advertising

The company in our simulation executes a multi-platform offline advertising program, including television, magazines, and radio. This brand drives a very large amount of online volume from offline advertising.

Be sure to enter "0.00" into all cells in B341 - B580.

Copy the values from D347 - D352, D395 - D400, and D443 - D448 into B347 - B352, B395 - B400, and B443 - B448.

We are ready to evaluate how customers acquired via Offline marketing perform. Let's review overall performance.

Table #18:   Customers Acquired via Offline Marketing

The Online Marketing Simulation: 240 Segment Analysis					
	Year 1	Year 2	Year 3	Year 4	Year 5
Change in Retention	1.00	1.00	1.00	1.00	1.00
Change in Acquisition	1.00	0.00	0.00	0.00	0.00
Change in Spend	1.00	1.00	1.00	1.00	1.00
	Year 1	Year 2	Year 3	Year 4	Year 5
Total Buyers On File	28,938	28,938	28,938	28,938	28,938
Total 12 Month Buyers	28,938	8,563	6,529	5,214	4,283
Total New Buyers	28,938	0	0	0	0
Total Demand	$6,001,223	$2,593,759	$2,070,435	$1,673,506	$1,382,532
Total Orders	39,165	15,454	11,971	9,697	8,019
Total Items	108,201	49,313	39,811	32,669	27,174
Orders per Buyer	1.353	1.805	1.834	1.860	1.872
Items per Order	2.763	3.191	3.326	3.369	3.389
Price per Item	$55.46	$52.60	$52.01	$51.23	$50.88
Average Order Value	$153.23	$167.84	$172.95	$172.58	$172.40
Demand per Buyer	$207.38	$302.90	$317.12	$320.95	$322.81
Total Customers = "A"	3,966	4,397	3,744	3,091	2,589
Total Customers = "B"	17,763	4,900	3,631	2,896	2,370
Total Customers = "C"	7,209	12,483	5,691	4,122	3,342
Total Customers = "D"	0	7,157	11,737	8,086	5,668
Total Customers = "F"	0	0	4,135	10,742	14,969

In our example, buyers acquired via offline advertising generate far more demand, long-term, than do customers acquired via affiliate marketing. If we sum the total demand line for years two through five, and divide it by the 28,938 newly acquired buyers, we obtain $266.79 of future demand, far greater than then $171 obtained via affiliate marketing.

Many of the metrics are different. The offline advertising customer tends to buy more expensive items, especially early in the purchase cycle. More customers stay in grades of "A", "B", and "C" compared with customers acquired via affiliate marketing.

Now let's look at how demand evolves across advertising micro-channels and merchandise divisions.

Table #19: Offline Ad Customers, Demand Trends

Demand by Segmentation Indicators					
Indicator	Year 1	Year 2	Year 3	Year 4	Year 5
Affiliates	$22,906	$98,381	$94,839	$82,000	$71,015
Offline Ads	$5,433,078	$1,186,103	$861,070	$647,434	$509,269
E-Mail	$210,368	$598,758	$509,468	$439,508	$377,697
Soc. Media	$45,730	$23,173	$19,869	$15,921	$13,235
Print Ads	$45,636	$21,621	$18,057	$16,514	$14,450
Search	$68,767	$174,178	$141,086	$119,107	$98,455
No Source	$174,739	$491,545	$426,047	$353,022	$298,411
Merch Div 1	$1,165,067	$506,813	$388,099	$305,821	$248,946
Merch Div 2	$1,233,048	$477,225	$398,991	$329,805	$272,922
Merch Div 3	$1,874,359	$779,011	$606,947	$481,251	$394,190
Merch Div 4	$696,767	$253,181	$203,220	$165,537	$137,700
Merch Div 5	$1,031,983	$577,529	$473,177	$391,092	$328,774
Demand	$6,001,223	$2,593,759	$2,070,435	$1,673,506	$1,382,532
Margin	$3,567,975	$1,427,195	$1,127,946	$904,006	$742,877

Trends are beginning to emerge. The customer stays loyal to offline advertising over time, but demand clearly shifts to e-mail marketing and organically to the website (no source).

Once again, there is a clear, long-term preference for these customers in merchandise division #3 and merchandise division #5.

We've established the fact that customers acquired via offline advertising are more valuable than are customers acquired via affiliate marketing. Now let's take a look at customers who purchase for the first time because of e-mail marketing.

E-Mail Marketing

This brand allows customers to opt-in to twice-weekly e-mail marketing campaigns. This allows the brand to generate a list of "prospect" customers, if you will. Eventually, some of the prospects click through the e-mail marketing campaigns and purchase for the first time. Let's see how these customers evolve and change over time.

Be sure to enter "0.00" into all cells in B341 - B580.

Copy the values from D353 - D358, D401 - D406, and D449 - D454 into B353 - B358, B401 - B406, and B449 - B454.

Let's see what happens!

Table #20: Customers Acquired via E-Mail Marketing

The Online Marketing Simulation: 240 Segment Analysis					
	Year 1	Year 2	Year 3	Year 4	Year 5
Change in Retention	1.00	1.00	1.00	1.00	1.00
Change in Acquisition	1.00	0.00	0.00	0.00	0.00
Change in Spend	1.00	1.00	1.00	1.00	1.00
	Year 1	Year 2	Year 3	Year 4	Year 5
Total Buyers On File	20,025	20,025	20,025	20,025	20,025
Total 12 Month Buyers	20,025	6,926	5,387	4,336	3,563
Total New Buyers	20,025	0	0	0	0
Total Demand	$4,842,965	$2,139,733	$1,710,892	$1,386,363	$1,143,639
Total Orders	34,206	13,673	10,617	8,514	6,966
Total Items	106,296	45,650	35,943	28,987	23,806
Orders per Buyer	1.708	1.974	1.971	1.964	1.955
Items per Order	3.108	3.339	3.385	3.405	3.418
Price per Item	$45.56	$46.87	$47.60	$47.83	$48.04
Average Order Value	$141.58	$156.50	$161.14	$162.84	$164.18
Demand per Buyer	$241.85	$308.95	$317.62	$319.74	$320.98
Total Customers = "A"	4,539	4,126	3,366	2,734	2,256
Total Customers = "B"	11,802	3,792	2,897	2,360	1,950
Total Customers = "C"	3,684	8,564	4,670	3,448	2,816
Total Customers = "D"	0	3,543	7,031	5,515	4,185
Total Customers = "F"	0	0	2,061	5,968	8,817

We've found the most valuable customers, so far! Summing demand in years two through five, dividing by 20,025 new customers, we get a future demand value of $318.63. We retain 35% of the customers in year two (6,926 / 20,025).

Notice that these customers buy less expensive items than do customers from affiliate marketing or from offline ads. This probably has something to do with the marketing strategy in the e-mail marketing program. If less expensive items are advertised, then you get customers who buy less expensive items! You will want to do this research in your business, to see if this trend happens across your customer base.

Success happens not because of expensive items, but because the customers have a much greater chance of repurchasing in the next twelve months. In other words, the e-mail marketing program cultivates a list of prospects that have a preference for the brand. The repeated exposure to the brand, through e-mail marketing, yields customers who are more loyal once they buy. Furthermore, once a customer buys, the customer is being constantly marketed to via e-mail marketing, whereas customers from other marketing channels (i.e. affiliates) may not sign up for e-mail marketing, and as a result, may forget that the brand even exists!

This is the success of e-mail marketing, a success that is almost never talked about by e-mail marketing experts. A combination of relationship marketing and demand generation yields high-value long-term customers, customers that have virtually zero incremental variable marketing cost. By using an Online Marketing Simulation, you get to compare the e-mail customer against all other sources of customers, and you get to see the incremental value appear right in front of your eyes!

Now we'll review micro-channel and merchandise division demand evolution.

Table #21: E-Mail Customer Demand Evolution

Demand by Segmentation Indicators					
Indicator	Year 1	Year 2	Year 3	Year 4	Year 5
Affiliates	$18,045	$83,246	$75,808	$67,901	$60,549
Offline Ads	$215,468	$437,415	$391,680	$336,643	$287,467
E-Mail	$4,125,999	$1,119,102	$799,040	$600,646	$468,657
Soc. Media	$71,606	$12,853	$12,176	$10,558	$9,037
Print Ads	$112,257	$17,766	$15,993	$14,669	$13,167
Search	$80,376	$73,255	$73,797	$66,307	$59,336
No Source	$219,215	$396,096	$342,398	$289,638	$245,426
Merch Div 1	$848,061	$377,141	$304,139	$245,694	$201,347
Merch Div 2	$1,037,104	$410,160	$321,126	$262,349	$218,195
Merch Div 3	$1,402,477	$599,532	$478,798	$387,955	$319,042
Merch Div 4	$485,093	$219,810	$171,543	$138,520	$114,230
Merch Div 5	$1,070,229	$533,090	$435,285	$351,844	$290,824
Demand	$4,842,965	$2,139,733	$1,710,892	$1,386,363	$1,143,639
Margin	$2,436,267	$1,063,575	$859,441	$699,450	$580,140

In our example, we see that offline ads, e-mail marketing, and organic online demand (no source) are the micro-channels that capture the majority of demand over time. Pay attention to merchandise division #2. E-mail marketing drives more customers to merchandise division #2 than do affiliate marketing or offline ads. Over time, the impact of merchandise division #2 is lessened, as merchandise divisions #3 and #5 gain the majority of future demand. Let's keep this fact in mind, given that the e-mail customer has the best long-term demand value, over time. Might the relationship between long-term value and merchandise division #2 also hold?

Social Media

This brand also tracks which social media site customers come from when they purchase, then groups all visitors under the label 'Social Media'. Let's see how social media customers migrate through the ecosystem.

Be sure to enter "0.00" into all cells in B341 - B580.

Copy the values from D359 - D364, D407 - D412, and D455 - D460 into B359 - B364, B407 - B412, and B455 - B460.

Table #22: Customers Acquired via Social Media

The Online Marketing Simulation: 240 Segment Analysis					
	Year 1	Year 2	Year 3	Year 4	Year 5
Change in Retention	1.00	1.00	1.00	1.00	1.00
Change in Acquisition	1.00	0.00	0.00	0.00	0.00
Change in Spend	1.00	1.00	1.00	1.00	1.00
	Year 1	Year 2	Year 3	Year 4	Year 5
Total Buyers On File	23,901	23,901	23,901	23,901	23,901
Total 12 Month Buyers	23,901	3,190	2,306	1,771	1,464
Total New Buyers	23,901	0	0	0	0
Total Demand	$2,036,168	$710,332	$582,198	$488,757	$424,864
Total Orders	25,623	5,008	3,823	3,074	2,589
Total Items	67,845	16,157	12,561	10,347	8,838
Orders per Buyer	1.072	1.570	1.658	1.736	1.768
Items per Order	2.648	3.226	3.285	3.365	3.414
Price per Item	$30.01	$43.97	$46.35	$47.24	$48.07
Average Order Value	$79.47	$141.84	$152.27	$158.98	$164.12
Demand per Buyer	$85.19	$222.67	$252.43	$276.01	$290.22
Total Customers = "A"	414	778	872	832	755
Total Customers = "B"	14,190	2,064	1,460	1,064	865
Total Customers = "C"	9,297	10,600	1,745	1,446	1,170
Total Customers = "D"	0	10,459	13,647	6,532	3,612
Total Customers = "F"	0	0	6,177	14,027	17,499

Customers acquired via social media have marginal long-term value, far worse, in fact, than those acquired via affiliate marketing. These customers spend $2.2 million in the four years after being acquired. When divided by 23,091 buyers, we find that these customers are worth a paltry $92.30 in the next four years. Only 3,190 of the 23,901 buyers purchase again in the second year, yielding a repurchase rate of just 13%. Also notice that social media customers are acquired at a price per item of about $30, significantly lower than the overall average. The social media customer at this brand quickly migrates to a grade of "F", and stays there.

Let's see if we can discern anything from a review of future demand by advertising micro-channel and merchandise division.

Table #23: Future Demand Trends, Social Media Customers

Demand by Segmentation Indicators					
Indicator	Year 1	Year 2	Year 3	Year 4	Year 5
Affiliates	$2,088	$34,416	$36,101	$32,364	$27,724
Offline Ads	$16,062	$181,614	$161,904	$131,755	$118,803
E-Mail	$29,013	$257,798	$185,454	$154,921	$132,064
Soc. Media	$1,957,445	$26,532	$15,086	$12,209	$8,474
Print Ads	$7,473	$33,890	$21,417	$16,424	$10,996
Search	$4,824	$44,385	$36,617	$30,460	$27,083
No Source	$19,263	$131,697	$125,618	$110,624	$99,720
Merch Div 1	$331,744	$122,519	$100,425	$83,813	$74,543
Merch Div 2	$1,082,539	$168,940	$138,488	$117,602	$100,140
Merch Div 3	$219,618	$177,137	$150,272	$125,911	$109,897
Merch Div 4	$185,374	$69,592	$55,221	$45,659	$40,284
Merch Div 5	$216,893	$172,145	$137,792	$115,773	$100,000
Demand	$2,036,168	$710,332	$582,198	$488,757	$424,864
Margin	$984,307	$357,190	$297,590	$254,335	$222,427

The social media shopper quickly migrates away from social media, and if the customer purchases again, the customer likes to focus on e-mail marketing and offline ads.

Pay close attention to the merchandise preferred by this customer, over time. When acquired, the customer spends about half of the demand in merchandise division #2. Recall that we surmised that merchandise division #2 might yield high-value customers, based on what we saw in our analysis of e-mail customers. This trend doesn't hold here, does it?

It is obvious that the customer acquired via social media, especially through merchandise division #2, does not migrate to high-value status. If the customers are referred to the website at little or no cost, then the business can harvest any incremental profit that is available. Otherwise, this business should not market to these customers in the future unless marketing comes with little cost.

Print Ads

This brand has specific print ads that invite the customer to purchase specific, popular items at a discount. Let's see how the print ad customer behaves.

Be sure to enter "0.00" into all cells in B341 - B580.

Copy the values from D365 - D370, D413 - D418, and D461 - D466 into B365 - B370, B413 - B418, and B461 - B466.

Table #24: Future Value of Print Ad Buyers

The Online Marketing Simulation: 240 Segment Analysis					
	Year 1	Year 2	Year 3	Year 4	Year 5
Change in Retention	1.00	1.00	1.00	1.00	1.00
Change in Acquisition	1.00	0.00	0.00	0.00	0.00
Change in Spend	1.00	1.00	1.00	1.00	1.00
	Year 1	Year 2	Year 3	Year 4	Year 5
Total Buyers On File	47,013	47,013	47,013	47,013	47,013
Total 12 Month Buyers	47,013	7,367	5,551	4,404	3,666
Total New Buyers	47,013	0	0	0	0
Total Demand	$3,718,496	$1,403,002	$1,245,724	$1,108,381	$980,278
Total Orders	50,133	10,779	8,527	7,189	6,209
Total Items	153,651	36,341	29,174	24,637	21,260
Orders per Buyer	1.066	1.463	1.536	1.632	1.694
Items per Order	3.065	3.371	3.421	3.427	3.424
Price per Item	$24.20	$38.61	$42.70	$44.99	$46.11
Average Order Value	$74.17	$130.16	$146.09	$154.18	$157.87
Demand per Buyer	$79.10	$190.44	$224.42	$251.68	$267.37
Total Customers = "A"	537	1,658	1,880	1,861	1,728
Total Customers = "B"	28,125	5,049	3,668	2,766	2,234
Total Customers = "C"	18,351	20,815	4,408	3,527	2,904
Total Customers = "D"	0	19,490	26,255	13,725	7,928
Total Customers = "F"	0	0	10,802	25,133	32,218

These customers aren't worth a whole lot, either!
Remember, these customers are getting a significant
discount on the merchandise they purchase, as evidenced
by the $24.20 average price of an item purchased when the
customer is acquired. Average order values are
exceptionally low in the acquisition year.

Notice that only 7,367 of the 47,013 buyers repurchase in
the next twelve months, a repurchase rate of about 16%.
During the next four years, these customers generate
$100.77 of demand, lower than average.

Let's review future advertising micro-channel and
merchandise division habits.

Table #25: Future Demand Trends, Print Ads

Demand by Segmentation Indicators					
Indicator	Year 1	Year 2	Year 3	Year 4	Year 5
Affiliates	$1,380	$70,294	$75,465	$69,312	$59,134
Offline Ads	$14,484	$293,373	$317,378	$297,251	$270,427
E-Mail	$31,442	$490,284	$402,781	$355,990	$311,515
Soc. Media	$8,383	$41,400	$31,558	$22,197	$16,479
Print Ads	$3,645,036	$194,971	$106,394	$66,715	$49,118
Search	$1,622	$48,320	$53,035	$56,564	$53,083
No Source	$16,149	$264,360	$259,114	$240,352	$220,521
Merch Div 1	$34,454	$128,965	$140,056	$140,805	$133,189
Merch Div 2	$3,369,717	$554,757	$443,510	$350,392	$286,289
Merch Div 3	$89,822	$325,925	$306,066	$283,980	$255,995
Merch Div 4	$197,748	$131,158	$111,381	$102,116	$92,870
Merch Div 5	$26,754	$262,198	$244,710	$231,089	$211,935
Demand	$3,718,496	$1,403,002	$1,245,724	$1,108,381	$980,278
Margin	$1,680,350	$691,630	$641,451	$576,903	$513,604

We've observed customers as they migrate from their original micro-channel to offline ads, e-mail, and organic website orders (no source). This example is not different. Also notice that these customers purchase almost exclusively from merchandise division #2 at first, then migrate across all merchandise divisions over time. This time, merchandise division #2 delivers lower-than-average value customers.

Paid Search

The paid search customer is always worth analyzing. Let's see what these customers deliver to the brand, over time.

Be sure to enter "0.00" into all cells in B341 – B580.

Copy the values from D371 – D376, D419 – D424, and D467 – D472 into B371 – B376, B419 – B424, and B467 – B472.

Table #26: Future Value of Paid Search Customers

The Online Marketing Simulation: 240 Segment Analysis					
	Year 1	Year 2	Year 3	Year 4	Year 5
Change in Retention	1.00	1.00	1.00	1.00	1.00
Change in Acquisition	1.00	0.00	0.00	0.00	0.00
Change in Spend	1.00	1.00	1.00	1.00	1.00
	Year 1	Year 2	Year 3	Year 4	Year 5
Total Buyers On File	14,217	14,217	14,217	14,217	14,217
Total 12 Month Buyers	14,217	2,935	2,042	1,543	1,204
Total New Buyers	14,217	0	0	0	0
Total Demand	$2,433,376	$807,524	$600,160	$476,906	$383,589
Total Orders	16,842	5,065	3,631	2,830	2,271
Total Items	44,124	15,429	11,995	9,476	7,671
Orders per Buyer	1.185	1.726	1.778	1.835	1.886
Items per Order	2.620	3.046	3.304	3.348	3.378
Price per Item	$55.15	$52.34	$50.03	$50.33	$50.00
Average Order Value	$144.48	$159.42	$165.29	$168.51	$168.91
Demand per Buyer	$171.16	$275.16	$293.88	$309.16	$318.54
Total Customers = "A"	1,101	1,084	964	827	695
Total Customers = "B"	8,739	1,840	1,229	903	689
Total Customers = "C"	4,377	6,224	1,742	1,259	1,003
Total Customers = "D"	0	5,070	7,088	3,592	2,075
Total Customers = "F"	0	0	3,193	7,637	9,754

The paid search customer exhibits very different behaviors. First of all, the paid search customer is purchasing at price points that are considerably higher than are customers who purchase in other advertising micro-channels ($55.15). 2,935 of the 14,217 first-year buyers purchase again in year two, yielding a 20% repurchase rate. Notice that the paid search customer is buying few items per order than customers acquired from other advertising micro-channels purchase. In other words, for this business, paid search appears to attract customers who buy fewer, but more expensive items. And there is a bit of good news. The $2.3 million in demand generated by these customers over the next four years yields a future demand value of $159.54.

Table #27: Future Demand Trends of Paid Search Customers

Demand by Segmentation Indicators					
Indicator	Year 1	Year 2	Year 3	Year 4	Year 5
Affiliates	$5,651	$29,780	$31,872	$29,341	$27,216
Offline Ads	$50,585	$219,641	$173,893	$140,128	$110,242
E-Mail	$61,959	$220,519	$169,910	$136,061	$113,958
Soc. Media	$11,225	$11,276	$10,688	$5,798	$3,877
Print Ads	$7,566	$7,353	$5,453	$5,401	$4,250
Search	$2,247,568	$156,737	$77,918	$52,628	$36,832
No Source	$48,821	$162,218	$130,427	$107,549	$87,214
Merch Div 1	$531,735	$151,363	$111,999	$87,623	$68,460
Merch Div 2	$529,250	$165,176	$115,525	$89,787	$70,947
Merch Div 3	$710,534	$224,468	$165,449	$130,833	$106,268
Merch Div 4	$240,567	$75,976	$57,506	$46,387	$37,585
Merch Div 5	$421,290	$190,542	$149,681	$122,275	$100,330
Demand	$2,433,376	$807,524	$600,160	$476,906	$383,589
Margin	$1,412,316	$441,736	$318,210	$252,373	$200,941

The paid search customer buys from all merchandise divisions, and eventually evolves behavior into merchandise division #3 and merchandise division #5. Like most other customers, the paid search buyer migrates into offline ads and e-mail. Still, a significant minority of demand is generated in year two from search. Google is smiling, once again!! All customers who purchase from this business have a predisposition to use search in the future, regardless of source of acquisition, building an unavoidable future expense commitment.

No Source of Acquisition

Now let's review all of the customers who are acquired organically, in other words, customers who we cannot definitively track to an original source. Intuitively, we might believe that these customers have a chance to have a decent level of future value, because the customer didn't just stumble across the website by accident, right? Something had to happen (word of mouth, social media, brand recognition, previous advertising) to cause this customer to purchase.

Be sure to enter "0.00" into all cells in B341 – B580.

Copy the values from D377 – D382, D425 – D430, and D473 – D478 into B377 – B382, B425 – B430, and B473 – B478.

Table #28: Future Value of "No Source" Customers

The Online Marketing Simulation: 240 Segment Analysis					
	Year 1	Year 2	Year 3	Year 4	Year 5
Change in Retention	1.00	1.00	1.00	1.00	1.00
Change in Acquisition	1.00	0.00	0.00	0.00	0.00
Change in Spend	1.00	1.00	1.00	1.00	1.00
	Year 1	Year 2	Year 3	Year 4	Year 5
Total Buyers On File	31,650	31,650	31,650	31,650	31,650
Total 12 Month Buyers	31,650	7,524	5,063	3,918	3,123
Total New Buyers	31,650	0	0	0	0
Total Demand	$6,935,854	$2,239,866	$1,531,820	$1,205,686	$977,758
Total Orders	41,162	12,702	8,838	7,030	5,733
Total Items	134,393	44,534	30,542	24,227	19,763
Orders per Buyer	1.301	1.688	1.746	1.794	1.836
Items per Order	3.265	3.506	3.456	3.446	3.447
Price per Item	$51.61	$50.30	$50.16	$49.77	$49.47
Average Order Value	$168.50	$176.34	$173.33	$171.49	$170.56
Demand per Buyer	$219.14	$297.68	$302.56	$307.70	$313.12
Total Customers = "A"	4,305	3,204	2,597	2,167	1,821
Total Customers = "B"	21,714	4,700	3,006	2,272	1,779
Total Customers = "C"	5,631	16,000	5,502	3,474	2,664
Total Customers = "D"	0	7,746	15,777	9,388	5,667
Total Customers = "F"	0	0	4,769	14,349	19,719

Sure enough, these customers have a reasonable amount of long-term value. 7,524 of the 31,650 first time buyers purchase again in the next twelve months, for a repurchase rate of 24%. These customers purchase items that are a bit more expensive than average, and buy more than three items per order. The $6.0 million of demand spent during the next four years yields a future demand value of $188.16, better than most of the customer segments we've analyzed.

Let's see how these customers migrate across advertising micro-channels and merchandise divisions.

Table #29: Future Demand Trends of "No Source" Customers

Demand by Segmentation Indicators					
Indicator	Year 1	Year 2	Year 3	Year 4	Year 5
Affiliates	$47,899	$113,585	$91,541	$80,100	$68,107
Offline Ads	$162,254	$648,077	$445,154	$348,563	$283,489
E-Mail	$220,037	$598,961	$432,730	$355,935	$294,149
Soc. Media	$48,069	$19,086	$12,784	$11,058	$9,300
Print Ads	$73,738	$19,478	$18,227	$14,776	$12,343
Search	$65,195	$133,828	$105,445	$79,014	$65,157
No Source	$6,318,661	$706,851	$425,939	$316,240	$245,213
Merch Div 1	$1,155,005	$384,715	$254,621	$198,469	$161,060
Merch Div 2	$1,751,422	$469,079	$316,772	$249,793	$198,933
Merch Div 3	$2,204,652	$717,655	$479,997	$365,881	$290,929
Merch Div 4	$599,976	$196,208	$135,087	$111,854	$93,629
Merch Div 5	$1,224,800	$472,210	$345,344	$279,690	$233,208
Demand	$6,935,854	$2,239,866	$1,531,820	$1,205,686	$977,758
Margin	$3,828,595	$1,180,677	$803,535	$630,733	$510,211

These customers do skew a bit to merchandise division #3 (and to a lesser extent, merchandise division #2) in their first year, but then eventually buy from both merchandise division #3 and merchandise division #5. The trend of the customer evolving merchandise preference to merchandise divisions #3 and #5 appears to hold, regardless of advertising micro-channel. These customers migrate to offline ads and e-mail marketing, replicating the trend we've observed over and over again.

Chapter 7: Future Value

Our analysis indicates that customers acquired from different micro-channels have different levels of future value.
- Affiliate Marketing = $171.14
- Offline Ads = $266.79
- E-Mail Marketing = $318.63
- Social Media = $92.30
- Print Ads = $100.77
- Paid Search = $159.54
- No Source = $188.16
- Overall Weighted Average = $192.01

It is obvious that customers acquired via e-mail marketing and offline ads have the best future value. It makes sense that the repeated impact of e-mail marketing campaigns and offline ads result in prospects that are more "fully developed" by the time the prospect decides to purchase for the first time.

Honestly, your results will be different than these. But I'm willing to bet that some of what is observed here holds for your business as well. The future of a healthy e-commerce business involves recruiting "prospects", folks who have not yet purchased but are in some way engaged with your brand. Over time, the prospect is converted to a customer, and then, over time, the customer becomes a loyal shopper. This is the classic marketing funnel we've all grown to know and love. Our job is to get much better at the "prospect to customer" stage, not necessarily demanding a conversion today, but instead, building a relationship that ultimately results in a purchase.

The concept of long-term value is not new to classic direct marketers. The folks who managed direct mail and catalog marketing programs have been practicing long-term value studies for decades. In online marketing, however, the focus is disproportionately on optimizing conversion rates.

The goal of any future value analysis is to combine the best aspects of optimizing conversion rate with a long-term customer value study. By focusing on both parts of the profitability equation, a business has the potential for short-term profitability and long-term success. Online Marketing Simulations help us achieve this opportunity.

Next, we will combine the long-term value of advertising micro-channels with the long-term value of customers who purchase from various merchandise divisions.

Chapter 8: Merchandise Preference

Any Online Marketing Simulation requires a review of customers who are acquired via various merchandise divisions. As much as we love optimizing our websites, executing tests, managing online marketing programs, and tracking social media, it is a given that merchandise is the differentiator. Merchandise is the reason a customer purchases from us. Knowing how a customer is likely to migrate through merchandise divisions, and knowing the merchandise divisions that yield high-value customers results in marketing strategies that grow the business over time.

Let's step through each of the five merchandise divisions, learning how customers who buy from each division evolve over time.

Merchandise Division #1

Be sure to enter "0.00" into all cells in B341 - B580.

Copy the values from column D into column B whenever you see a segment that ends in "MD1", in the range of B341 - B580.

Table #30: Future Value of Merchandise Division #1 Buyers

The Online Marketing Simulation: 240 Segment Analysis					
	Year 1	Year 2	Year 3	Year 4	Year 5
Change in Retention	1.00	1.00	1.00	1.00	1.00
Change in Acquisition	1.00	0.00	0.00	0.00	0.00
Change in Spend	1.00	1.00	1.00	1.00	1.00
	Year 1	Year 2	Year 3	Year 4	Year 5
Total Buyers On File	24,261	24,261	24,261	24,261	24,261
Total 12 Month Buyers	24,261	5,033	3,556	2,722	2,153
Total New Buyers	24,261	0	0	0	0
Total Demand	$3,327,575	$1,287,825	$978,535	$772,791	$636,022
Total Orders	30,744	9,297	6,638	5,137	4,116
Total Items	71,931	27,816	20,799	16,333	13,303
Orders per Buyer	1.267	1.847	1.867	1.887	1.911
Items per Order	2.340	2.992	3.133	3.179	3.232
Price per Item	$46.26	$46.30	$47.05	$47.32	$47.81
Average Order Value	$108.23	$138.53	$147.41	$150.43	$154.53
Demand per Buyer	$137.16	$255.86	$275.14	$283.90	$295.34
Total Customers = "A"	2,184	2,179	1,814	1,492	1,240
Total Customers = "B"	15,300	3,087	2,128	1,598	1,244
Total Customers = "C"	6,777	11,664	3,485	2,377	1,855
Total Customers = "D"	0	7,331	12,069	6,229	3,594
Total Customers = "F"	0	0	4,765	12,564	16,328

Here are some of the key metrics. About 21% of these customers purchase again in the next twelve months (5,033 / 24,261). These customers purchase average price points, and buy a slightly smaller number of items per order than the average customer. Over the course of four years, these customers spend $3.7 million dollars, yielding a future demand value of $151.48.

Next, we review the advertising micro-channels and merchandise divisions that these customers eventually migrate through.

Table #31: Future Demand, Merchandise Division #1

Demand by Segmentation Indicators					
Indicator	Year 1	Year 2	Year 3	Year 4	Year 5
Affiliates	$186,900	$78,505	$58,829	$45,867	$37,318
Offline Ads	$815,539	$420,977	$319,124	$246,634	$199,738
E-Mail	$593,463	$392,006	$302,553	$247,561	$207,052
Soc. Media	$320,758	$13,881	$12,469	$9,761	$7,719
Print Ads	$33,242	$6,701	$7,870	$7,497	$6,513
Search	$487,476	$113,170	$76,414	$57,876	$46,731
No Source	$890,198	$262,586	$201,276	$157,595	$130,952
Merch Div 1	$2,908,391	$567,045	$348,745	$241,966	$177,629
Merch Div 2	$80,483	$121,432	$119,825	$106,591	$95,099
Merch Div 3	$125,314	$224,298	$200,255	$170,447	$150,556
Merch Div 4	$85,448	$88,183	$74,175	$64,876	$56,475
Merch Div 5	$127,939	$286,867	$235,535	$188,911	$156,264
Demand	$3,327,575	$1,287,825	$978,535	$772,791	$636,022
Margin	$1,550,650	$610,837	$476,155	$381,219	$317,617

A disproportionate number of customers appear to be sourced via search. Notice that customers who purchase from merchandise division #1 are still more loyal to merchandise division #1 over time than to any other merchandise division. However, by year five, these customers have spread across the entire brand, buying from all merchandise divisions.

Merchandise Division #2

Be sure to enter "0.00" into all cells in B341 - B580.

Copy the values from column D into column B whenever you see a segment that ends in "MD2", in the range of B341 - B580.

Table #32: Future Value of Merchandise Division #2 Buyers

The Online Marketing Simulation: 240 Segment Analysis					
	Year 1	Year 2	Year 3	Year 4	Year 5
Change in Retention	1.00	1.00	1.00	1.00	1.00
Change in Acquisition	1.00	0.00	0.00	0.00	0.00
Change in Spend	1.00	1.00	1.00	1.00	1.00
	Year 1	Year 2	Year 3	Year 4	Year 5
Total Buyers On File	82,989	82,989	82,989	82,989	82,989
Total 12 Month Buyers	82,989	14,845	11,188	8,936	7,390
Total New Buyers	82,989	0	0	0	0
Total Demand	$8,687,438	$3,319,592	$2,807,712	$2,419,924	$2,097,711
Total Orders	93,252	22,369	17,750	14,926	12,752
Total Items	278,685	75,907	61,001	51,370	43,970
Orders per Buyer	1.124	1.507	1.587	1.670	1.726
Items per Order	2.989	3.393	3.437	3.442	3.448
Price per Item	$31.17	$43.73	$46.03	$47.11	$47.71
Average Order Value	$93.16	$148.40	$158.18	$162.13	$164.51
Demand per Buyer	$104.68	$223.62	$250.95	$270.80	$283.87
Total Customers = "A"	3,132	4,582	4,600	4,268	3,824
Total Customers = "B"	49,827	9,811	7,082	5,431	4,379
Total Customers = "C"	30,030	36,712	9,438	7,227	5,908
Total Customers = "D"	0	31,884	43,551	23,180	13,752
Total Customers = "F"	0	0	18,318	42,884	55,126

Alright folks, we have 82,989 customers who place a first order with a preference for merchandise division #2. These customers spend $10.6 million over the next four years, yielding a future demand value of just $128.27. Notice that just 18% of the 82,989 buyers purchase again in the next twelve months. The average price per item is low, at $31.17.

Things don't look so good for merchandise division #2.

Let's see how demand evolves over time.

Table #33: Future Demand, Merchandise Division #2

Demand by Segmentation Indicators					
Indicator	Year 1	Year 2	Year 3	Year 4	Year 5
Affiliates	$159,511	$169,022	$159,676	$143,102	$123,990
Offline Ads	$1,005,699	$841,637	$770,986	$676,738	$598,325
E-Mail	$765,217	$1,093,037	$881,741	$764,564	$657,723
Soc. Media	$1,223,396	$73,752	$53,475	$40,587	$30,693
Print Ads	$3,581,152	$252,975	$148,247	$99,812	$72,906
Search	$489,356	$156,384	$145,928	$131,880	$120,373
No Source	$1,463,108	$732,785	$647,660	$563,242	$493,701
Merch Div 1	$100,154	$320,039	$327,683	$308,404	$289,284
Merch Div 2	$7,790,868	$1,395,456	$1,021,835	$789,668	$626,081
Merch Div 3	$294,137	$781,966	$704,916	$631,081	$556,155
Merch Div 4	$447,589	$263,312	$236,187	$212,992	$191,743
Merch Div 5	$54,691	$558,819	$517,090	$477,780	$434,446
Demand	$8,687,438	$3,319,592	$2,807,712	$2,419,924	$2,097,711
Margin	$4,657,762	$1,755,909	$1,501,543	$1,293,802	$1,119,770

What is interesting is that print ads are such a huge portion of the story here. Recall that print ad customers had very low future demand value. One has to wonder if it is merchandise division #2 that is the problem, or if print ads are the problem? We'll tackle that issue later in the book.

Notice that customers do stay loyal to merchandise division #2, spending more in this division than any other.

Merchandise Division #3

Be sure to enter "0.00" into all cells in B341 – B580.

Copy the values from column D into column B whenever you see a segment that ends in "MD3", in the range of B341 – B580.

Table #34: Future Value of Merchandise Division #1 Buyers

The Online Marketing Simulation: 240 Segment Analysis					
	Year 1	Year 2	Year 3	Year 4	Year 5
Change in Retention	1.00	1.00	1.00	1.00	1.00
Change in Acquisition	1.00	0.00	0.00	0.00	0.00
Change in Spend	1.00	1.00	1.00	1.00	1.00
	Year 1	Year 2	Year 3	Year 4	Year 5
Total Buyers On File	32,118	32,118	32,118	32,118	32,118
Total 12 Month Buyers	32,118	8,742	6,224	4,788	3,863
Total New Buyers	32,118	0	0	0	0
Total Demand	$6,338,586	$2,642,910	$1,914,715	$1,509,476	$1,223,742
Total Orders	43,932	15,658	11,343	8,882	7,203
Total Items	120,417	50,427	37,173	29,602	24,263
Orders per Buyer	1.368	1.791	1.822	1.855	1.865
Items per Order	2.741	3.221	3.277	3.333	3.368
Price per Item	$52.64	$52.41	$51.51	$50.99	$50.44
Average Order Value	$144.28	$168.79	$168.80	$169.95	$169.89
Demand per Buyer	$197.35	$302.32	$307.62	$315.29	$316.78
Total Customers = "A"	4,356	3,999	3,300	2,699	2,241
Total Customers = "B"	21,123	5,006	3,502	2,691	2,169
Total Customers = "C"	6,639	14,512	5,318	3,795	3,040
Total Customers = "D"	0	8,601	14,931	9,228	6,002
Total Customers = "F"	0	0	5,068	13,704	18,666

This information looks more promising, doesn't it? The 32,118 customers purchasing from merchandise division #3 have a 27% retention rate from year one to year 2 (8,742 / 32,118). The $7.3 million spent by the 32,118 customers yields a future demand value of $227.00! Customers are purchasing merchandise at higher price points, and are still buying a reasonably high number of items per order.

Table #35: Future Trends, Merchandise Division #3

Demand by Segmentation Indicators					
Indicator	Year 1	Year 2	Year 3	Year 4	Year 5
Affiliates	$360,608	$158,824	$113,546	$94,042	$78,046
Offline Ads	$1,653,611	$832,064	$603,108	$465,474	$371,418
E-Mail	$1,224,307	$820,580	$607,776	$483,969	$392,676
Soc. Media	$244,050	$20,008	$15,241	$12,672	$10,470
Print Ads	$117,473	$19,675	$15,466	$13,070	$12,154
Search	$707,145	$183,264	$126,133	$99,593	$81,696
No Source	$2,031,391	$608,496	$433,446	$340,655	$277,281
Merch Div 1	$254,085	$328,975	$264,534	$219,955	$184,907
Merch Div 2	$456,045	$401,810	$312,636	$258,185	$217,284
Merch Div 3	$5,149,954	$1,308,777	$840,242	$598,534	$451,581
Merch Div 4	$383,559	$215,485	$162,100	$133,700	$112,599
Merch Div 5	$94,944	$387,862	$335,202	$299,103	$257,371
Demand	$6,338,586	$2,642,910	$1,914,715	$1,509,476	$1,223,742
Margin	$3,461,360	$1,402,603	$1,007,554	$791,853	$640,897

The customers buying from merchandise division #3 are likely to buy online, without attribution. Over time, customers continue to prefer merchandise division #3, and predictably, the customer migrates to offline ads, e-mail marketing, and buying online without attribution to any other marketing micro-channel.

These customers appear to have good long-term value!

Merchandise Division #4

Be sure to enter "0.00" into all cells in B341 - B580.

Copy the values from column D into column B whenever you see a segment that ends in "MD4", in the range of B341 - B580.

Table #36: Future Value of Merchandise Division #4 Buyers

The Online Marketing Simulation: 240 Segment Analysis					
	Year 1	Year 2	Year 3	Year 4	Year 5
Change in Retention	1.00	1.00	1.00	1.00	1.00
Change in Acquisition	1.00	0.00	0.00	0.00	0.00
Change in Spend	1.00	1.00	1.00	1.00	1.00
	Year 1	Year 2	Year 3	Year 4	Year 5
Total Buyers On File	9,108	9,108	9,108	9,108	9,108
Total 12 Month Buyers	9,108	2,064	1,507	1,184	957
Total New Buyers	9,108	0	0	0	0
Total Demand	$893,766	$475,763	$394,856	$340,942	$281,989
Total Orders	11,394	3,735	2,746	2,196	1,789
Total Items	32,778	12,428	9,375	7,684	6,190
Orders per Buyer	1.251	1.810	1.823	1.854	1.869
Items per Order	2.877	3.328	3.414	3.499	3.459
Price per Item	$27.27	$38.28	$42.12	$44.37	$45.56
Average Order Value	$78.44	$127.38	$143.79	$155.26	$157.60
Demand per Buyer	$98.13	$230.55	$262.08	$287.87	$294.56
Total Customers = "A"	525	743	693	610	522
Total Customers = "B"	5,007	1,206	869	671	544
Total Customers = "C"	3,576	3,628	1,149	904	742
Total Customers = "D"	0	3,532	4,206	2,198	1,364
Total Customers = "F"	0	0	2,191	4,724	5,937

New customers purchasing from merchandise division #4 seem to be pretty average, or a bit below average. 2,064 of 9,108 customers purchase again within twelve months, yielding an annual retention rate of 23%. The customers spend $1.5 million over the course of the next four years, yielding a future demand value of $163.98. This low value is probably driven by the very low price per item purchased ($27.27).

Table #37: Future Demand, Merchandise Division #4

Demand by Segmentation Indicators					
Indicator	Year 1	Year 2	Year 3	Year 4	Year 5
Affiliates	$46,762	$22,549	$22,576	$20,887	$17,459
Offline Ads	$242,517	$162,626	$130,258	$107,976	$87,371
E-Mail	$181,631	$173,910	$129,732	$107,308	$89,906
Soc. Media	$35,863	$4,110	$3,952	$3,326	$2,604
Print Ads	$25,934	$7,740	$6,446	$5,408	$4,046
Search	$122,175	$27,463	$25,913	$25,961	$21,016
No Source	$238,885	$77,365	$75,979	$70,077	$59,587
Merch Div 1	$27,849	$70,293	$66,226	$59,650	$49,027
Merch Div 2	$52,061	$71,619	$67,875	$60,190	$50,222
Merch Div 3	$46,715	$98,595	$89,247	$82,373	$72,233
Merch Div 4	$759,802	$157,032	$94,096	$66,085	$47,617
Merch Div 5	$7,340	$78,223	$77,412	$72,644	$62,890
Demand	$893,766	$475,763	$394,856	$340,942	$281,989
Margin	$606,833	$271,342	$219,319	$185,979	$151,982

Customers purchasing from merchandise division #4 migrate to merchandise division #3 and merchandise division #5. In fact, it looks like customers purchasing from merchandise division #4 are least likely to remain loyal to their merchandise division. Customers buying from merchandise division #4 are a cross-section of all advertising micro-channels.

Merchandise Division #5

Be sure to enter "0.00" into all cells in B341 - B580.

Copy the values from column D into column B whenever you see a segment that ends in "MD5", in the range of B341 - B580.

Table #38: Future Value of Merchandise Division #5 Buyers

The Online Marketing Simulation: 240 Segment Analysis					
	Year 1	Year 2	Year 3	Year 4	Year 5
Change in Retention	1.00	1.00	1.00	1.00	1.00
Change in Acquisition	1.00	0.00	0.00	0.00	0.00
Change in Spend	1.00	1.00	1.00	1.00	1.00
	Year 1	Year 2	Year 3	Year 4	Year 5
Total Buyers On File	13,509	13,509	13,509	13,509	13,509
Total 12 Month Buyers	13,509	3,885	2,732	2,113	1,716
Total New Buyers	13,509	0	0	0	0
Total Demand	$4,282,407	$1,360,257	$951,901	$728,896	$589,995
Total Orders	20,286	7,529	5,304	4,110	3,353
Total Items	57,189	24,050	17,500	13,730	11,284
Orders per Buyer	1.502	1.938	1.941	1.945	1.954
Items per Order	2.819	3.195	3.300	3.340	3.365
Price per Item	$74.88	$56.56	$54.39	$53.09	$52.29
Average Order Value	$211.10	$180.68	$179.48	$177.33	$175.96
Demand per Buyer	$317.00	$350.13	$348.45	$344.94	$343.88
Total Customers = "A"	2,916	2,220	1,685	1,340	1,103
Total Customers = "B"	8,829	2,142	1,489	1,150	931
Total Customers = "C"	1,764	6,472	2,810	1,858	1,446
Total Customers = "D"	0	2,674	6,137	4,584	3,159
Total Customers = "F"	0	0	1,388	4,577	6,870

This looks like a good merchandise division, doesn't it? 3,885 of the 13,509 customers buying in year one buy again in year two, resulting in an annual repurchase rate of 29%. The $3.6 million spent by these customers in the next four years yields a future demand value of $268.79. Customers who purchase from this merchandise division tend to buy expensive items, spending $74.88 per item in the year the customer is acquired. Even better, the customer still buys 2.8 items per order, propping up the average order value.

Table #39: Future Demand, Merchandise Division #5

Demand by Segmentation Indicators					
Indicator	Year 1	Year 2	Year 3	Year 4	Year 5
Affiliates	$357,887	$96,094	$66,252	$51,675	$44,282
Offline Ads	$955,772	$379,985	$278,885	$211,002	$170,242
E-Mail	$1,025,121	$447,639	$311,753	$237,355	$189,990
Soc. Media	$249,169	$18,478	$11,548	$7,515	$5,774
Print Ads	$71,629	$10,698	$7,359	$6,513	$5,665
Search	$421,554	$100,542	$66,731	$51,099	$40,272
No Source	$1,201,275	$306,820	$209,374	$163,737	$133,771
Merch Div 1	$281,672	$229,017	$160,129	$124,106	$99,803
Merch Div 2	$184,866	$139,400	$111,649	$95,575	$83,229
Merch Div 3	$224,124	$199,428	$171,447	$143,298	$122,205
Merch Div 4	$126,681	$98,590	$74,401	$60,237	$50,608
Merch Div 5	$3,465,064	$693,821	$434,276	$305,680	$234,151
Demand	$4,282,407	$1,360,257	$951,901	$728,896	$589,995
Margin	$2,105,513	$669,812	$468,213	$361,433	$294,371

This table is interesting. Notice that the customers who purchase from merchandise division #5 are generally acquired via e-mail marketing and organic e-commerce (no source). Customers do stay loyal to merchandise division #5 over time, with dollars also flowing into merchandise division #3.

Future Value, By Merchandise Division

We now have a profile of future demand value by merchandise division. Let's review what we learned.
- Merchandise Division #1 = $151.48
- Merchandise Division #2 = $128.27
- Merchandise Division #3 = $227.00
- Merchandise Division #4 = $163.98
- Merchandise Division #5 = $268.79

Also interesting is the average price point spent by customers during their acquisition year.

- Merchandise Division #1 = $46.26
- Merchandise Division #2 = $31.17
- Merchandise Division #3 = $52.64
- Merchandise Division #4 = $27.77
- Merchandise Division #5 = $74.88

There is a correlation between the price point that a new customer tends to purchase, and the future value generated by the new customer. This is an important point. Direct marketers have known for a long time that it is important to generate as large an average order value as possible on a first order, because the future demand generated by customers spending a lot on a first order is better than is generated by customers spending less on a first order.

And yet, in e-commerce, the opposite strategy is often practiced. Customers are given incentives and discounts and promotions to "encourage" the prospect to purchase, right now!

Use Online Marketing Simulations to identify the advertising micro-channels and merchandise divisions that yield highly valuable customers. Once you have the information from a series of simulations, calibrate customer acquisition activities around the high-value combinations, populating the customer base with really good, productive, valuable buyers that guarantee the long-term viability of your business!

Chapter 9: Print Ads and Merchandise Division #2

The simulations suggest that the combination of print ads and merchandise division is not good at generating new customers that are likely to come back and spend a lot in the future.

So let's do an experiment.

Be sure to enter "0.00" into all cells in B341 – B580.

Now, we're going to analyze how newly acquired e-mail customers perform across merchandise divisions. In other words, we will analyze each combination, hopefully giving us insight into the merchandise divisions that yield high-value customers within e-mail marketing.

Start the process by populating B353, B401, and B449 with the contents of cells D353, D401, and D449.

Table #40: Future Value, E-Mail and Merchandise Div. #1

The Online Marketing Simulation: 240 Segment Analysis					
	Year 1	Year 2	Year 3	Year 4	Year 5
Change in Retention	1.00	1.00	1.00	1.00	1.00
Change in Acquisition	1.00	0.00	0.00	0.00	0.00
Change in Spend	1.00	1.00	1.00	1.00	1.00
	Year 1	Year 2	Year 3	Year 4	Year 5
Total Buyers On File	3,351	3,351	3,351	3,351	3,351
Total 12 Month Buyers	3,351	1,032	808	628	505
Total New Buyers	3,351	0	0	0	0
Total Demand	$548,439	$242,631	$209,967	$174,640	$146,535
Total Orders	5,172	2,010	1,557	1,228	985
Total Items	13,449	5,852	4,775	3,886	3,185
Orders per Buyer	1.543	1.947	1.927	1.955	1.952
Items per Order	2.600	2.912	3.068	3.164	3.232
Price per Item	$40.78	$41.46	$43.97	$44.94	$46.00
Average Order Value	$106.04	$120.72	$134.87	$142.19	$148.69
Demand per Buyer	$163.66	$235.04	$259.88	$277.91	$290.29
Total Customers = "A"	516	538	451	369	303
Total Customers = "B"	2,085	607	461	353	282
Total Customers = "C"	750	1,518	728	516	409
Total Customers = "D"	0	688	1,293	918	642
Total Customers = "F"	0	0	419	1,195	1,714

For this combination, 31% of customers repurchase in year two. Customers spend $773,000 demand in the next four years, for a future demand value of $230.91.

Now it is time for the all-important combination of e-mail and merchandise division #2.

Be sure to enter "0.00" into all cells in B341 – B580.

Populate B354, B402, and B450 with the contents of cells D354, D402, and D450.

Table #41: Future Value, E-Mail and Merchandise Div. #2

The Online Marketing Simulation: 240 Segment Analysis					
	Year 1	Year 2	Year 3	Year 4	Year 5
Change in Retention	1.00	1.00	1.00	1.00	1.00
Change in Acquisition	1.00	0.00	0.00	0.00	0.00
Change in Spend	1.00	1.00	1.00	1.00	1.00
	Year 1	Year 2	Year 3	Year 4	Year 5
Total Buyers On File	3,627	3,627	3,627	3,627	3,627
Total 12 Month Buyers	3,627	1,085	854	693	570
Total New Buyers	3,627	0	0	0	0
Total Demand	$700,245	$306,590	$249,582	$209,690	$176,213
Total Orders	5,094	1,753	1,433	1,222	1,033
Total Items	15,720	6,181	5,030	4,279	3,612
Orders per Buyer	1.404	1.616	1.678	1.764	1.811
Items per Order	3.086	3.526	3.510	3.502	3.496
Price per Item	$44.54	$49.60	$49.62	$49.01	$48.78
Average Order Value	$137.46	$174.89	$174.17	$171.61	$170.52
Demand per Buyer	$193.06	$282.66	$292.26	$302.76	$308.89
Total Customers = "A"	525	551	480	407	345
Total Customers = "B"	2,355	644	489	394	321
Total Customers = "C"	747	1,733	835	572	460
Total Customers = "D"	0	699	1,423	1,049	737
Total Customers = "F"	0	0	401	1,205	1,765

Take a look at this, folks! Merchandise division #2 doesn't look so bad, when viewed through the eyes of customers who purchased via e-mail marketing. 1,085 of the 3,627 first time buyers purchase again within twelve months, for a repurchase rate of 30%. These customers spend $942,000 in the next four years, for a future demand value of $259.74.

In other words, the problem isn't with merchandise division #2. The problem is that merchandise division #2 is offered in print ads, and the print ads attract customers who want the special promotion in the print ad, not a relationship with the brand.

Let's continue the exercise, moving on to merchandise division #3.

Be sure to enter "0.00" into all cells in B341 - B580.

Populate B355, B403, and B451 with the contents of cells D355, D403, and D451.

Table #42: Future Value, E-Mail and Merchandise Div. #3

The Online Marketing Simulation: 240 Segment Analysis					
	Year 1	Year 2	Year 3	Year 4	Year 5
Change in Retention	1.00	1.00	1.00	1.00	1.00
Change in Acquisition	1.00	0.00	0.00	0.00	0.00
Change in Spend	1.00	1.00	1.00	1.00	1.00
	Year 1	Year 2	Year 3	Year 4	Year 5
Total Buyers On File	5,088	5,088	5,088	5,088	5,088
Total 12 Month Buyers	5,088	1,643	1,286	1,047	860
Total New Buyers	5,088	0	0	0	0
Total Demand	$1,088,392	$489,198	$392,669	$320,762	$266,222
Total Orders	7,965	3,029	2,401	1,947	1,602
Total Items	23,466	9,815	7,911	6,500	5,429
Orders per Buyer	1.565	1.844	1.866	1.860	1.863
Items per Order	2.946	3.241	3.295	3.338	3.389
Price per Item	$46.38	$49.84	$49.64	$49.35	$49.03
Average Order Value	$136.65	$161.51	$163.56	$164.72	$166.17
Demand per Buyer	$213.91	$297.78	$305.23	$306.37	$309.58
Total Customers = "A"	948	870	722	590	493
Total Customers = "B"	3,291	919	718	599	493
Total Customers = "C"	849	2,337	1,119	803	664
Total Customers = "D"	0	961	1,990	1,461	1,051
Total Customers = "F"	0	0	538	1,635	2,387

Merchandise division #3 customers are good customers, as evidenced by an annual year one to year two retention rate of (1,643 / 5,088) 32%, spending $1.5 million over the next four years, for a future demand value of $288.69.

Merchandise division #4 will be analyzed next.

Be sure to enter "0.00" into all cells in B341 – B580.

Populate B356, B404, and B452 with the contents of cells D356, D404, and D452.

Table #43: Future Value, E-Mail and Merchandise Div. #4

The Online Marketing Simulation: 240 Segment Analysis					
	Year 1	Year 2	Year 3	Year 4	Year 5
Change in Retention	1.00	1.00	1.00	1.00	1.00
Change in Acquisition	1.00	0.00	0.00	0.00	0.00
Change in Spend	1.00	1.00	1.00	1.00	1.00
	Year 1	Year 2	Year 3	Year 4	Year 5
Total Buyers On File	1,818	1,818	1,818	1,818	1,818
Total 12 Month Buyers	1,818	568	424	325	262
Total New Buyers	1,818	0	0	0	0
Total Demand	$164,294	$141,459	$114,513	$93,989	$78,602
Total Orders	2,499	1,150	852	647	518
Total Items	7,449	3,962	2,915	2,231	1,775
Orders per Buyer	1.375	2.024	2.011	1.992	1.979
Items per Order	2.981	3.445	3.423	3.450	3.428
Price per Item	$22.06	$35.71	$39.29	$42.14	$44.29
Average Order Value	$65.74	$123.00	$134.47	$145.37	$151.81
Demand per Buyer	$90.37	$248.95	$270.36	$289.63	$300.40
Total Customers = "A"	132	226	209	178	151
Total Customers = "B"	900	299	229	175	143
Total Customers = "C"	786	646	292	231	191
Total Customers = "D"	0	647	652	373	261
Total Customers = "F"	0	0	436	860	1,072

The trends continue to be somewhat similar. The retention rate, from year one to year two is 31% (568 / 1,818). Customers spend $429,000 over the next four years, yielding a future demand value of $235.73.

Merchandise division #5 wraps-up this portion of the analysis.

Be sure to enter "0.00" into all cells in B341 - B580.

Populate B357, B405, and B453 with the contents of cells D357, D405, and D453.

Table #44: Future Value, E-Mail and Merchandise Div. #5

The Online Marketing Simulation: 240 Segment Analysis					
	Year 1	Year 2	Year 3	Year 4	Year 5
Change in Retention	1.00	1.00	1.00	1.00	1.00
Change in Acquisition	1.00	0.00	0.00	0.00	0.00
Change in Spend	1.00	1.00	1.00	1.00	1.00
	Year 1	Year 2	Year 3	Year 4	Year 5
Total Buyers On File	2,835	2,835	2,835	2,835	2,835
Total 12 Month Buyers	2,835	1,035	762	611	504
Total New Buyers	2,835	0	0	0	0
Total Demand	$936,078	$360,826	$273,260	$211,445	$170,820
Total Orders	4,899	2,087	1,558	1,226	1,004
Total Items	13,536	6,696	5,201	4,114	3,376
Orders per Buyer	1.728	2.016	2.045	2.005	1.991
Items per Order	2.763	3.209	3.337	3.357	3.363
Price per Item	$69.15	$53.88	$52.54	$51.39	$50.60
Average Order Value	$191.08	$172.90	$175.34	$172.51	$170.16
Demand per Buyer	$330.19	$348.52	$358.65	$345.96	$338.72
Total Customers = "A"	765	646	502	396	325
Total Customers = "B"	1,704	547	396	329	275
Total Customers = "C"	366	1,240	677	476	389
Total Customers = "D"	0	402	1,063	922	702
Total Customers = "F"	0	0	197	712	1,144

Merchandise division #5 has good performance, and performance within e-mail marketing is no exception! 1,035 of 2,853 customers are retained in year two, for an annual retention rate of 37%. Customers spend $1,016,000 over the next four years, delivering a four year demand value of $358.50 per customer.

Let's review customer performance across merchandise divisions within customers who were acquired via e-mail marketing.
- Merchandise Division #1 = $230.91
- Merchandise Division #2 = $259.74
- Merchandise Division #3 = $288.69
- Merchandise Division #4 = $235.73
- Merchandise Division #5 = $358.50

Merchandise division #2 is not the worst merchandise division at delivering customers with good long-term value within e-mail marketing. In fact, merchandise division #2 ranked third out of five merchandise divisions.

Why would I go to such lengths to demonstrate this outcome?

It is my opinion that modern e-commerce practitioners have not been given the tools to understand the complex interactions that occur between advertising micro-channels, merchandise divisions, and customers. Everything in e-commerce is predicated on a "conversion", taking whatever steps are necessary to get a customer to purchase, right now. We offer discounts and promotions and incentives, we try to cross-sell and up-sell, we try to make navigation easy, we try to make sure subject lines are compelling and keywords are selected at the lowest possible cost coupled with the highest possible conversion.

Online Marketing Simulations show us that long-term business success is predicated on making wise choices when acquiring customers. We must be thoughtful about how we acquire customers, carefully considering the advertising micro-channels that yield long-term value, coupled with a merchandise offering that results in a happy, loyal customer that wants to purchase in the future.

Chapter 10: Most Valuable Path

Not many e-commerce marketers talk about the concept of the "Most Valuable Path", or "MVP".

The objective is to find the route that customers take as they migrate from first-time buyer status to becoming a loyal customer.

We know that customers acquired via offline ads and e-mail marketing have superior future value. The data suggests that merchandise division #3 and merchandise division #5 yield customers with superior value. We know that new customers enter with an average grade of "B" or "C".

So let's try something. Let's analyze customers who have a grade of "B", and let's do a comparison.

Re-open the spreadsheet, and enter "0.00" in to cells C6 – G6. Next, enter "0.00" into cells B101 – B340.

Now, go down to cell B157, and enter the value "1,000". We are going to simulate how 1,000 customers with a grade of "B", a preference for offline ads, and a preference for merchandise division #3 perform.

Table #45: Grade = "B", Offline Ads, Merchandise Div. #3

The Online Marketing Simulation: 240 Segment Analysis					
	Year 1	Year 2	Year 3	Year 4	Year 5
Change in Retention	1.00	1.00	1.00	1.00	1.00
Change in Acquisition	0.00	0.00	0.00	0.00	0.00
Change in Spend	1.00	1.00	1.00	1.00	1.00
	Year 1	Year 2	Year 3	Year 4	Year 5
Total Buyers On File	1,000	1,000	1,000	1,000	1,000
Total 12 Month Buyers	297	219	168	137	116
Total New Buyers	0	0	0	0	0
Total Demand	$80,097	$65,295	$53,025	$43,556	$36,913
Total Orders	512	384	308	254	215
Total Items	1,559	1,237	1,031	852	725
Orders per Buyer	1.725	1.754	1.835	1.854	1.852
Items per Order	3.043	3.220	3.345	3.363	3.368
Price per Item	$51.39	$52.78	$51.45	$51.09	$50.90
Average Order Value	$156.37	$169.98	$172.10	$171.81	$171.42
Demand per Buyer	$269.69	$298.08	$315.83	$318.55	$317.47
Total Customers = "A"	112	109	92	78	67
Total Customers = "B"	171	125	95	76	65
Total Customers = "C"	585	181	129	104	87
Total Customers = "D"	132	508	319	207	148
Total Customers = "F"	0	76	365	534	633

Customers with these attributes, over the course of five years, generate $278,886 demand (sum cells C13 - G13).

Next, enter "0" into cell B157, and enter "1,000" into cell B163. We're going to simulate how 1,000 customers with e-mail preference perform, over the next five years.

Table #46: Grade = "B", E-Mail, Merchandise Div. #3

The Online Marketing Simulation: 240 Segment Analysis					
	Year 1	Year 2	Year 3	Year 4	Year 5
Change in Retention	1.00	1.00	1.00	1.00	1.00
Change in Acquisition	0.00	0.00	0.00	0.00	0.00
Change in Spend	1.00	1.00	1.00	1.00	1.00
	Year 1	Year 2	Year 3	Year 4	Year 5
Total Buyers On File	1,000	1,000	1,000	1,000	1,000
Total 12 Month Buyers	293	236	197	162	138
Total New Buyers	0	0	0	0	0
Total Demand	$71,066	$66,967	$58,046	$49,266	$42,326
Total Orders	482	418	355	297	253
Total Items	1,486	1,361	1,178	1,005	867
Orders per Buyer	1.643	1.772	1.805	1.832	1.839
Items per Order	3.086	3.253	3.317	3.380	3.424
Price per Item	$47.81	$49.20	$49.28	$49.02	$48.79
Average Order Value	$147.55	$160.04	$163.45	$165.66	$167.07
Demand per Buyer	$242.38	$283.64	$295.07	$303.43	$307.29
Total Customers = "A"	112	120	105	90	78
Total Customers = "B"	186	137	116	95	80
Total Customers = "C"	583	226	152	126	106
Total Customers = "D"	118	450	311	212	160
Total Customers = "F"	0	66	316	478	576

Total demand over five years is $278,671, very similar to what we observed with offline ads.

Let's run a simulation for paid search, just to understand if search continues to lag behind in long-term value. Zero-out cell B163, and enter "1,000" into cell B181.

Table #47: Grade = "B", Search, Merchandise Div. #3

The Online Marketing Simulation: 240 Segment Analysis					
	Year 1	Year 2	Year 3	Year 4	Year 5
Change in Retention	1.00	1.00	1.00	1.00	1.00
Change in Acquisition	0.00	0.00	0.00	0.00	0.00
Change in Spend	1.00	1.00	1.00	1.00	1.00
	Year 1	Year 2	Year 3	Year 4	Year 5
Total Buyers On File	1,000	1,000	1,000	1,000	1,000
Total 12 Month Buyers	234	153	121	94	76
Total New Buyers	0	0	0	0	0
Total Demand	$62,222	$43,277	$37,659	$30,102	$24,195
Total Orders	378	276	224	178	144
Total Items	1,127	880	722	585	476
Orders per Buyer	1.615	1.802	1.858	1.891	1.891
Items per Order	2.983	3.190	3.227	3.288	3.313
Price per Item	$55.23	$49.16	$52.12	$51.43	$50.82
Average Order Value	$164.75	$156.83	$168.20	$169.08	$168.37
Demand per Buyer	$266.02	$282.59	$312.45	$319.75	$318.42
Total Customers = "A"	72	74	68	56	46
Total Customers = "B"	159	91	66	51	41
Total Customers = "C"	600	132	94	76	62
Total Customers = "D"	170	599	300	168	112
Total Customers = "F"	0	105	474	649	739

We again validate that paid search customers have lower value, generating $197,455 over five years.

Now it is time for an interesting tidbit. Zero-out cell B181, and enter "1,000" into cell B193. These customers prefer multiple advertising micro-channels.

Table #48: Grade = "B", Multiple Chan., Merchandise Div. #3

The Online Marketing Simulation: 240 Segment Analysis					
	Year 1	Year 2	Year 3	Year 4	Year 5
Change in Retention	1.00	1.00	1.00	1.00	1.00
Change in Acquisition	0.00	0.00	0.00	0.00	0.00
Change in Spend	1.00	1.00	1.00	1.00	1.00
	Year 1	Year 2	Year 3	Year 4	Year 5
Total Buyers On File	1,000	1,000	1,000	1,000	1,000
Total 12 Month Buyers	332	295	244	199	163
Total New Buyers	0	0	0	0	0
Total Demand	$93,403	$95,314	$81,450	$67,166	$54,938
Total Orders	556	544	467	387	318
Total Items	1,744	1,854	1,590	1,319	1,086
Orders per Buyer	1.675	1.844	1.917	1.943	1.952
Items per Order	3.134	3.407	3.405	3.410	3.416
Price per Item	$53.56	$51.41	$51.23	$50.92	$50.60
Average Order Value	$167.86	$175.12	$174.45	$173.65	$172.89
Demand per Buyer	$281.16	$322.98	$334.48	$337.41	$337.49
Total Customers = "A"	194	190	162	133	109
Total Customers = "B"	166	144	122	102	84
Total Customers = "C"	611	331	220	166	132
Total Customers = "D"	28	325	368	326	270
Total Customers = "F"	0	10	129	273	405

This is the fabled "multi-channel" customer finding that we read about in the multichannel marketing literature. Customers who prefer multiple advertising micro-channels spend $392,271 across five years.

In other words, we've found a change in the path that leads to greater value. Good for us!

And if this works for advertising micro-channels, it should work for multiple merchandise divisions, shouldn't it? Enter "0" into cell B193, and then enter "1,000" into cell B196. This segment of customers purchased from multiple advertising micro-channels, and purchased from multiple merchandise divisions. Let's see what happens!

Table #49: Grade = "B", Multiple Chan., Multiple Merch Div.

The Online Marketing Simulation: 240 Segment Analysis					
	Year 1	Year 2	Year 3	Year 4	Year 5
Change in Retention	1.00	1.00	1.00	1.00	1.00
Change in Acquisition	0.00	0.00	0.00	0.00	0.00
Change in Spend	1.00	1.00	1.00	1.00	1.00
	Year 1	Year 2	Year 3	Year 4	Year 5
Total Buyers On File	1,000	1,000	1,000	1,000	1,000
Total 12 Month Buyers	332	292	257	223	194
Total New Buyers	0	0	0	0	0
Total Demand	$82,386	$95,223	$87,222	$75,774	$65,131
Total Orders	546	567	516	449	388
Total Items	1,768	1,960	1,792	1,558	1,341
Orders per Buyer	1.644	1.945	2.006	2.010	1.998
Items per Order	3.238	3.457	3.474	3.469	3.460
Price per Item	$46.60	$48.57	$48.69	$48.63	$48.57
Average Order Value	$150.88	$167.93	$169.14	$168.69	$168.06
Demand per Buyer	$248.08	$326.54	$339.24	$339.05	$335.84
Total Customers = "A"	194	210	188	161	137
Total Customers = "B"	237	147	129	114	101
Total Customers = "C"	556	375	253	193	158
Total Customers = "D"	13	263	307	272	227
Total Customers = "F"	0	6	123	260	377

The results are even better! In this simulation, customers spend $405,737 over five years.

Take a look at column "D" in the spreadsheet, especially cells "D118" and "D148". These are the cells that have the biggest file counts within customers with a grade of "A". In both cases, customers buy from multiple merchandise divisions. In one case, the customer prefers e-mail marketing, in the other, the customer likes to shop from multiple advertising micro-channels.

It appears that we've identified a "Most Valuable Path", or "MVP":

- Build awareness via offline advertising or e-mail marketing, which causes a customer to purchase for the first time. Encourage the customer to purchase from merchandise division #3 or merchandise division #5.
- After a first purchase, encourage subsequent purchases from other merchandise divisions.
- After a first purchase, encourage a customer to purchase from other advertising micro-channels, or encourage customer to purchase via e-mail marketing.

Long-term success is predicated on encouraging customers to migrate along this path.

Chapter 11: Making "MVP" Actionable

It is time to convert all of this exciting information into something that is actionable for the aspiring web analyst and online marketer.

Recall what we learned about the four-year value of a newly acquired customer.
- Affiliate Marketing = $171.14
- Offline Ads = $266.79
- E-Mail Marketing = $318.63
- Social Media = $92.30
- Print Ads = $100.77
- Paid Search = $159.54
- No Source = $188.16
- Overall Weighted Average = $192.01

Let's assume that the CEO wants to optimize paid search marketing. The following table illustrates how data from the simulation is combined with actual campaign results.

Table #50: Paid Search, Short-Term And Long-Term Results

Paid Search Marketing Strategy	
Number of Clicks	20,000
Cost per Click	$0.65
Conversion Rate	1.00%
Total Buyers	200
Average Order Value	$144.48
Total Demand	$28,896
Flow-Through To Profit	37.0%
Contribution	$10,692
Less Advertising Cost	$13,000
Variable Operating Profit	($2,308)
Profit (Loss) Per New Customer	($11.54)
One-Year Future Demand	$56.80
One-Year Future Profit	$21.02
Net One Year Profit	$9.47
Four-Year Future Demand	$159.54
Four-Year Future Profit	$59.03
Net Four Year Profit	$47.49

From a "conversion rate" standpoint, this paid search campaign appears to be a failure, right? Look at the lousy results! Assuming that 37% of demand flows-through to profit, this campaign cost $13,000, and resulted in a loss of $2,308. When we divide the loss by the number of new customers, we learn that we lost $11.54 profit for every new customer we acquired.

So we failed.

Or did we?

The OMS suggests that paid search newbies generate $56.08 demand in the twelve months after a first purchase. At a 37% flow-through rate to profit, this means that each paid search newbie will generate $21.02 profit in the next year.

In other words, we lose $11.54 in the short-term, and generate $21.02 profit in the next year. The "relationship", if you will, is worth $9.47 profit!

The OMS proves that this level of paid search marketing is profitable, and worth doing. In fact, over the course of four years, the relationship is highly profitable, generating $47.49 of profit!

This is why we need to run Online Marketing Simulations. We must have the knowledge of the future, in order to correctly manage our campaigns. Armed with this data, the web analyst or online marketer visits the CEO, and asks for an increase in the marketing budget. Without this data, the CEO may cut your budget!

Let's say that you are able to double your paid search budget, now that you are armed with this data. What happens? Well, the results appear, on the surface, to be even worse than where the budget was originally set.

Table #51: Paid Search Budget Is Doubled

Paid Search Marketing Strategy	
Number of Clicks	40,000
Cost per Click	$0.65
Conversion Rate	0.81%
Total Buyers	325
Average Order Value	$144.48
Total Demand	$46,956
Flow-Through To Profit	37.0%
Contribution	$17,374
Less Advertising Cost	$26,000
Variable Operating Profit	($8,626)
Profit (Loss) Per New Customer	($26.54)
One-Year Future Demand	$56.80
One-Year Future Profit	$21.02
Net One Year Profit	($5.53)
Four-Year Future Demand	$159.54
Four-Year Future Profit	$59.03
Net Four Year Profit	$32.49

On a "conversion rate" basis, the campaign appears to be nothing short of apocalyptic! A terrible conversion rate yields a loss of $8,626, or a loss of $26.54 per new customer.

Oh boy.

The loss of $26.54 does not offset the $21.02 profit generated in the next twelve months.

Oh boy.

But look at four year profit. If your business can afford to acquire customers at a loss this significant, then your business will be rewarded over time with customers that continue to generate profit over time.

In other words, the knowledge derived from an Online Marketing Simulation causes a business to make _very different decisions_. Within paid search, we would happily pay more for keywords that drive customers to landing pages with merchandise from merchandise divisions three and five. These two merchandise divisions generate new customers that have better long-term value than do the other three merchandise divisions.

Each advertising micro-channel can be optimized via short-term conversion and long-term value. Without Online Marketing Simulations, you make decisions that are only optimal in the short-term.

Chapter 12: CEOs Ask Different Questions

I continually read marketing and analytics content that focuses on the phrase "optimization".

If you ask 100 online marketers or web analytics experts, you're likely to find ninety or more individuals who consider optimization within the confines of an individual transaction. In other words, the process of getting a customer to purchase something today is "optimized".

I have yet to find a CEO who wants me to "optimize" individual transactions. In all cases, CEOs ask me to balance short-term conversion metrics with long-term profitability. CEOs want to see how their business will evolve over time, given changes in short-term decisions.

It wasn't always like this. When e-commerce experienced unfettered growth, one didn't need to know the future trajectory of website sales, because it was easy to forecast growth, and if growth exceeded expectations, nobody cared! Now, the world has changed. Future e-commerce growth will be much harder to achieve. A CEO needs to know where the future is headed, and needs to have the tools that allow for long-term optimization.

As illustrated in this handbook, we make very different decisions when we understand how customers interact with advertising micro-channels and merchandise divisions. We use Online Marketing Simulations to illustrate the "MVP", or "Most Valuable Path" from acquisition to loyalty. Knowledge gained from and OMS project is used to significantly change how a business views individual campaigns. The goal isn't to optimize a campaign. The goal is to optimize the long-term health of a business. This is what a CEO wants to accomplish.

In other words, the OMS framework addresses the problems Sr. Management face. The OMS framework finally puts the web analytics expert or online marketing leader in a position of strategy. Individual tactics, while important, are viewed within the context of acquiring customers and managing existing customer relationships. The focus shifts from short-term optimization via technology and tactics to long-term profitability via customer relationships.

Not Just For Pure E-Commerce

The OMS framework, while presented from an e-commerce viewpoint, applies to any business model.

Web analytics data can be folded into the simulation at any step. Website visits, depth of visit, abandoned shopping carts, e-mail marketing click-throughs, and landing pages visited can all be folded into the model, enriching long-term customer understanding.

The social media brand can segment customers based on levels of engagement, update frequency, and level of connectivity with influential users.

A bank can integrate online bill paying with offline products purchased.

A subscription-based business utilizes Online Marketing Simulations for to track subscriber counts by month, over time.

A telecommunications brand can look at subscription information and utilization metrics to simulate a path to increasing the customer base.

In fact, you don't have to have any online data at all! The framework will help a retailer or catalog brand understand who is purchasing merchandise via offline marketing channels. The framework can easily be applied to any discipline.

The framework is nearly perfect for a Venture Capitalist looking to make an investment in a startup. We simply plug in customer data from the startup, and then forecast where the business might be heading, illustrating evolutionary trends that help the VC make proper investment decisions.

Similarly, the framework is applicable to Private Equity firms, helping them understand how distressed brands might eventually be rescued.

Business Owners like the OMS framework, especially when the owner is considering a sale of the brand. The OMS framework helps the owner understand where the business is headed, from a sales and profitability standpoint, so that an appropriate multiple of sales/profit can be determined.

Chapter 13: Encouragement

I am so excited about Online Marketing Simulations! I simply cannot wait to share this information with all Business Leaders, Online Marketers, and Web Analytics experts.

More than anything else, I want to help provide you with the tools necessary to make better decisions. An entire generation of business analysts and leaders were trained to focus on short-term results. Finally, we have a framework to think about business in a different way.

It has been my experience that individuals who have a keen knowledge of future customer behavior tend to be desired by Sr. Management. Anybody can tell the CEO about a campaign that resulted in a 2.14% conversion rate. Few people can tell the CEO that the campaign will result in $4,000,000 of long-term profit. I want you to be the individual who recommends changes in business strategy, based on future customer trends and past customer activities.

Honestly, it is time for e-commerce practitioners to be given tools that enable movement beyond technology and tactics. When building a website, technology and tactics are important. When sales are growing at an unfettered rate, technology and tactics are important. When business growth begins to slow, a thorough understanding of customer behavior is absolutely essential.

Most web analytics tools illustrate customer behavior within the context of a conversion. The OMS forecasts customer behavior over the next five years. When you know what is likely to happen in the future, you get to have a relationship with Sr. Management. This relationship exposes you to more business problems. The OMS framework, coupled with your web analytics solution, enable you to solve more problems, giving you more access to Sr. Management.

I've yet to work with a Sr. Management team that doesn't appreciate knowledge of the future. All of my Multichannel Forensics projects (the pre-cursor to OMS) result in forecasts of customer behavior. The forecast spreadsheets are always the most appreciated aspect of my projects, they always create the most conversation about potential business strategies.

I am thoroughly encouraged by your interest in Online Marketing Simulations! You have an interest in tools and techniques that enable you to make better business decisions. By reading this text, you are acknowledging that you need to know more about future customer behavior. That is a very, very good thing!

Have fun learning about customer behavior! Have an even better time applying what you learn to making better strategic decisions. Apply your results to individual marketing campaigns. Re-evaluate your simulation tool as time goes by, adding additional customer data as it becomes available.

And tell me what you learn! Evangelize the methodology, sharing the concepts with others. Let's take e-commerce and analytics in new and exciting directions. Let's discover how customers behave!

Appendix: Programming Code

I am including the SPSS code that I use to create an Online Marketing Simulation. This code is not elegant, well written, or even worthy of professional consideration. It simply gets the job done, and as far as I am concerned, that is all that matters.

I utilize what I call a "flat file", a dataset that has one row for every item a customer purchases. There are certain fields that are in every "flat file" that I analyze.
- Household_ID: Identifies who the customer is.
- Ord_Date: The date a customer ordered merchandise.
- Quantity: Number of items purchased.
- Demand: Total demand spent.
- Kev_Chan: Identifies the advertising micro-channel.
- Kev_Mrch: Identifies the merchandise division.
- Year: I group transactions into twelve-month buckets.

This is a really simple file layout. And with something so simple, an entire OMS spreadsheet can be created, a spreadsheet that clearly outlines how your business can grow profitably, well into the future.

The remainder of this book outlines the SPSS programming code that can be used to build the simulation. Feel free to convert the code to suit your own needs, and feel free to expand upon the existing 240 segment OMS framework.

```
*** Prepare The Datasets *** This Dataset Is The Dataset For Last Year ***.
get file = 'c:\datasets\OMS_Book.sav'.
select if demand gt 0.
select if quantity gt 0.
compute future = 0.
if (year = 2008)  future = demand.
compute rebuy  = 0.
if (future > 0)  rebuy = 1.
compute demd12 = 0.
compute demd99 = 0.
compute freq12 = 0.
compute freq99 = 0.
compute item12 = 0.
compute item99 = 0.
do if (year = 2007).
compute demd12 = demand.
compute freq12 = 1.
compute item12 = quantity.
end if.
do if (year < 2007).
compute demd99 = demand.
compute freq99 = 1.
compute item99 = quantity.
end if.
compute ind00 = 0.
compute ind01 = 0.
compute ind02 = 0.
compute ind03 = 0.
compute ind04 = 0.
compute ind05 = 0.
compute ind06 = 0.
compute ind07 = 0.
compute ind08 = 0.
compute ind09 = 0.
compute ind10 = 0.
compute ind11 = 0.
compute ind12 = 0.
compute ind13 = 0.
compute ind14 = 0.
compute ind15 = 0.
compute ind16 = 0.
compute ind17 = 0.
compute ind18 = 0.
compute ind19 = 0.
compute ind20 = 0.
compute ind21 = 0.
compute ind22 = 0.
compute ind23 = 0.
compute ind24 = 0.
compute ind25 = 0.
compute ind26 = 0.
compute ind27 = 0.
compute ind28 = 0.
compute ind29 = 0.
compute ind30 = 0.
compute ind31 = 0.
compute ind32 = 0.
compute ind33 = 0.
compute ind34 = 0.
compute ind35 = 0.
compute ind36 = 0.
compute ind37 = 0.
compute ind38 = 0.
compute ind39 = 0.
compute ind40 = 0.
compute ind41 = 0.
compute ind42 = 0.
```

```
compute ind43 = 0.
compute ind44 = 0.
compute ind45 = 0.
compute ind46 = 0.
compute ind47 = 0.
compute ind48 = 0.
compute ind49 = 0.
compute ind50 = 0.
compute ind51 = 0.
compute ind52 = 0.
compute ind53 = 0.
compute ind54 = 0.
compute ind55 = 0.
compute ind56 = 0.
compute ind57 = 0.
compute ind58 = 0.
compute ind59 = 0.
compute ind60 = 0.
compute ind61 = 0.
compute ind62 = 0.
compute ind63 = 0.
compute ind64 = 0.
compute ind65 = 0.
compute ind66 = 0.
compute ind67 = 0.
compute ind68 = 0.
compute ind69 = 0.
compute ind70 = 0.
compute ind71 = 0.
compute ind72 = 0.
compute ind73 = 0.
compute ind74 = 0.
compute ind75 = 0.
compute ind76 = 0.
compute ind77 = 0.
compute ind78 = 0.
compute ind79 = 0.
compute ind80 = 0.
compute ind81 = 0.
compute ind82 = 0.
compute ind83 = 0.
compute ind84 = 0.
compute ind85 = 0.
compute ind86 = 0.
compute ind87 = 0.
compute ind88 = 0.
compute ind89 = 0.
compute ind90 = 0.
compute ind91 = 0.
compute ind92 = 0.
compute ind93 = 0.
compute ind94 = 0.
compute ind95 = 0.
compute ind96 = 0.
compute ind97 = 0.
compute ind98 = 0.
compute ind99 = 0.
do if (year < 2008).
if (kev_chan = 06)  ind00 = demand.
if (kev_chan = 07)  ind01 = demand.
if (kev_chan = 08)  ind02 = demand.
if (kev_chan = 09)  ind03 = demand.
if (kev_chan = 10)  ind04 = demand.
if (kev_chan = 11)  ind05 = demand.
if (kev_chan = 12)  ind06 = demand.
if (kev_mrch = 01)  ind11 = demand.
if (kev_mrch = 02)  ind11 = demand.
```

```
if (kev_mrch = 03)   ind12 = demand.
if (kev_mrch = 04)   ind13 = demand.
if (kev_mrch = 05)   ind13 = demand.
if (kev_mrch = 06)   ind14 = demand.
if (kev_mrch = 07)   ind15 = demand.
if (kev_mrch = 08)   ind15 = demand.
if (kev_mrch = 09)   ind15 = demand.
if (kev_mrch = 10)   ind15 = demand.
if (kev_mrch = 11)   ind11 = demand.
compute              ind21 = demand.
compute              ind22 = gross_margin.
end if.
compute recency = 999.
if (ord_date gt 20071100) and (ord_date le 20071200)  recency = 001.
if (ord_date gt 20071000) and (ord_date le 20071100)  recency = 002.
if (ord_date gt 20070900) and (ord_date le 20071000)  recency = 003.
if (ord_date gt 20070800) and (ord_date le 20070900)  recency = 004.
if (ord_date gt 20070700) and (ord_date le 20070800)  recency = 005.
if (ord_date gt 20070600) and (ord_date le 20070700)  recency = 006.
if (ord_date gt 20070500) and (ord_date le 20070600)  recency = 007.
if (ord_date gt 20070400) and (ord_date le 20070500)  recency = 008.
if (ord_date gt 20070300) and (ord_date le 20070400)  recency = 009.
if (ord_date gt 20070200) and (ord_date le 20070300)  recency = 010.
if (ord_date gt 20070100) and (ord_date le 20070200)  recency = 011.
if (ord_date gt 20061200) and (ord_date le 20070100)  recency = 012.
if (ord_date gt 20061100) and (ord_date le 20061200)  recency = 013.
if (ord_date gt 20061000) and (ord_date le 20061100)  recency = 014.
if (ord_date gt 20060900) and (ord_date le 20061000)  recency = 015.
if (ord_date gt 20060800) and (ord_date le 20060900)  recency = 016.
if (ord_date gt 20060700) and (ord_date le 20060800)  recency = 017.
if (ord_date gt 20060600) and (ord_date le 20060700)  recency = 018.
if (ord_date gt 20060500) and (ord_date le 20060600)  recency = 019.
if (ord_date gt 20060400) and (ord_date le 20060500)  recency = 020.
if (ord_date gt 20060300) and (ord_date le 20060400)  recency = 021.
if (ord_date gt 20060200) and (ord_date le 20060300)  recency = 022.
if (ord_date gt 20060100) and (ord_date le 20060200)  recency = 023.
if (ord_date gt 20051200) and (ord_date le 20060100)  recency = 024.
if (ord_date gt 20051100) and (ord_date le 20051200)  recency = 025.
if (ord_date gt 20051000) and (ord_date le 20051100)  recency = 026.
if (ord_date gt 20050900) and (ord_date le 20051000)  recency = 027.
if (ord_date gt 20050800) and (ord_date le 20050900)  recency = 028.
if (ord_date gt 20050700) and (ord_date le 20050800)  recency = 029.
if (ord_date gt 20050600) and (ord_date le 20050700)  recency = 030.
if (ord_date gt 20050500) and (ord_date le 20050600)  recency = 031.
if (ord_date gt 20050400) and (ord_date le 20050500)  recency = 032.
if (ord_date gt 20050300) and (ord_date le 20050400)  recency = 033.
if (ord_date gt 20050200) and (ord_date le 20050300)  recency = 034.
if (ord_date gt 20050100) and (ord_date le 20050200)  recency = 035.
if (ord_date gt 20041200) and (ord_date le 20050100)  recency = 036.
if (ord_date gt 20041100) and (ord_date le 20041200)  recency = 037.
if (ord_date gt 20041000) and (ord_date le 20041100)  recency = 038.
if (ord_date gt 20040900) and (ord_date le 20041000)  recency = 039.
if (ord_date gt 20040800) and (ord_date le 20040900)  recency = 040.
if (ord_date gt 20040700) and (ord_date le 20040800)  recency = 041.
if (ord_date gt 20040600) and (ord_date le 20040700)  recency = 042.
if (ord_date gt 20040500) and (ord_date le 20040600)  recency = 043.
if (ord_date gt 20040400) and (ord_date le 20040500)  recency = 044.
if (ord_date gt 20040300) and (ord_date le 20040400)  recency = 045.
if (ord_date gt 20040200) and (ord_date le 20040300)  recency = 046.
if (ord_date gt 20040100) and (ord_date le 20040200)  recency = 047.
if (ord_date gt 20031200) and (ord_date le 20040100)  recency = 048.
aggregate outfile = *
        /presorted
        /break      = household_id ord_date
        /rebuy      = max(rebuy)
        /future     = sum(future)
        /recency    = min(recency)
```

```
        /demd12 demd99    = sum(demd12 demd99)
        /freq12 freq99    = max(freq12 freq99)
        /item12 item99    = sum(item12 item99)
        /ind00 ind01 ind02 ind03 ind04 ind05 ind06 ind07 ind08 ind09
         ind10 ind11 ind12 ind13 ind14 ind15 ind16 ind17 ind18 ind19
         ind20 ind21 ind22 ind23 ind24 ind25 ind26 ind27 ind28 ind29
         ind30 ind31 ind32 ind33 ind34 ind35 ind36 ind37 ind38 ind39
         ind40 ind41 ind42 ind43 ind44 ind45 ind46 ind47 ind48 ind49
         ind50 ind51 ind52 ind53 ind54 ind55 ind56 ind57 ind58 ind59
         ind60 ind61 ind62 ind63 ind64 ind65 ind66 ind67 ind68 ind69
         ind70 ind71 ind72 ind73 ind74 ind75 ind76 ind77 ind78 ind79
         ind80 ind81 ind82 ind83 ind84 ind85 ind86 ind87 ind88 ind89
         ind90 ind91 ind92 ind93 ind94 ind95 ind96 ind97 ind98 ind99 = sum
        (ind00 ind01 ind02 ind03 ind04 ind05 ind06 ind07 ind08 ind09
         ind10 ind11 ind12 ind13 ind14 ind15 ind16 ind17 ind18 ind19
         ind20 ind21 ind22 ind23 ind24 ind25 ind26 ind27 ind28 ind29
         ind30 ind31 ind32 ind33 ind34 ind35 ind36 ind37 ind38 ind39
         ind40 ind41 ind42 ind43 ind44 ind45 ind46 ind47 ind48 ind49
         ind50 ind51 ind52 ind53 ind54 ind55 ind56 ind57 ind58 ind59
         ind60 ind61 ind62 ind63 ind64 ind65 ind66 ind67 ind68 ind69
         ind70 ind71 ind72 ind73 ind74 ind75 ind76 ind77 ind78 ind79
         ind80 ind81 ind82 ind83 ind84 ind85 ind86 ind87 ind88 ind89
         ind90 ind91 ind92 ind93 ind94 ind95 ind96 ind97 ind98 ind99).
aggregate outfile = *
        /presorted
        /break          = household_id
        /rebuy          = max(rebuy)
        /future         = sum(future)
        /recency        = min(recency)
        /demd12 demd99    = sum(demd12 demd99)
        /freq12 freq99    = sum(freq12 freq99)
        /item12 item99    = sum(item12 item99)
        /ind00 ind01 ind02 ind03 ind04 ind05 ind06 ind07 ind08 ind09
         ind10 ind11 ind12 ind13 ind14 ind15 ind16 ind17 ind18 ind19
         ind20 ind21 ind22 ind23 ind24 ind25 ind26 ind27 ind28 ind29
         ind30 ind31 ind32 ind33 ind34 ind35 ind36 ind37 ind38 ind39
         ind40 ind41 ind42 ind43 ind44 ind45 ind46 ind47 ind48 ind49
         ind50 ind51 ind52 ind53 ind54 ind55 ind56 ind57 ind58 ind59
         ind60 ind61 ind62 ind63 ind64 ind65 ind66 ind67 ind68 ind69
         ind70 ind71 ind72 ind73 ind74 ind75 ind76 ind77 ind78 ind79
         ind80 ind81 ind82 ind83 ind84 ind85 ind86 ind87 ind88 ind89
         ind90 ind91 ind92 ind93 ind94 ind95 ind96 ind97 ind98 ind99 = sum
        (ind00 ind01 ind02 ind03 ind04 ind05 ind06 ind07 ind08 ind09
         ind10 ind11 ind12 ind13 ind14 ind15 ind16 ind17 ind18 ind19
         ind20 ind21 ind22 ind23 ind24 ind25 ind26 ind27 ind28 ind29
         ind30 ind31 ind32 ind33 ind34 ind35 ind36 ind37 ind38 ind39
         ind40 ind41 ind42 ind43 ind44 ind45 ind46 ind47 ind48 ind49
         ind50 ind51 ind52 ind53 ind54 ind55 ind56 ind57 ind58 ind59
         ind60 ind61 ind62 ind63 ind64 ind65 ind66 ind67 ind68 ind69
         ind70 ind71 ind72 ind73 ind74 ind75 ind76 ind77 ind78 ind79
         ind80 ind81 ind82 ind83 ind84 ind85 ind86 ind87 ind88 ind89
         ind90 ind91 ind92 ind93 ind94 ind95 ind96 ind97 ind98 ind99).
select if recency ne 999.
compute root_rec = sqrt(recency).
formats rebuy(f1.0) recency(f3.0) freq12 to freq99(f3.0) item12 to
item99(f3.0).
save outfile = 'c:\datasets\OMS1.sav'.
execute.


*** Prepare The Datasets *** This Dataset Is The Dataset For Next Year ***.
get file = 'c:\datasets\OMS_Book.sav'.
select if demand gt 0.
select if quantity gt 0.
compute future = 0.
if (year = 2009)  future = demand.
compute rebuy  = 0.
```

111

```
if (future > 0)  rebuy = 1.
compute demd12 = 0.
compute demd99 = 0.
compute freq12 = 0.
compute freq99 = 0.
compute item12 = 0.
compute item99 = 0.
do if (year = 2008).
compute demd12 = demand.
compute freq12 = 1.
compute item12 = quantity.
end if.
do if (year < 2008).
compute demd99 = demand.
compute freq99 = 1.
compute item99 = quantity.
end if.
compute ind00 = 0.
compute ind01 = 0.
compute ind02 = 0.
compute ind03 = 0.
compute ind04 = 0.
compute ind05 = 0.
compute ind06 = 0.
compute ind07 = 0.
compute ind08 = 0.
compute ind09 = 0.
compute ind10 = 0.
compute ind11 = 0.
compute ind12 = 0.
compute ind13 = 0.
compute ind14 = 0.
compute ind15 = 0.
compute ind16 = 0.
compute ind17 = 0.
compute ind18 = 0.
compute ind19 = 0.
compute ind20 = 0.
compute ind21 = 0.
compute ind22 = 0.
compute ind23 = 0.
compute ind24 = 0.
compute ind25 = 0.
compute ind26 = 0.
compute ind27 = 0.
compute ind28 = 0.
compute ind29 = 0.
compute ind30 = 0.
compute ind31 = 0.
compute ind32 = 0.
compute ind33 = 0.
compute ind34 = 0.
compute ind35 = 0.
compute ind36 = 0.
compute ind37 = 0.
compute ind38 = 0.
compute ind39 = 0.
compute ind40 = 0.
compute ind41 = 0.
compute ind42 = 0.
compute ind43 = 0.
compute ind44 = 0.
compute ind45 = 0.
compute ind46 = 0.
compute ind47 = 0.
compute ind48 = 0.
compute ind49 = 0.
```

```
compute ind50 = 0.
compute ind51 = 0.
compute ind52 = 0.
compute ind53 = 0.
compute ind54 = 0.
compute ind55 = 0.
compute ind56 = 0.
compute ind57 = 0.
compute ind58 = 0.
compute ind59 = 0.
compute ind60 = 0.
compute ind61 = 0.
compute ind62 = 0.
compute ind63 = 0.
compute ind64 = 0.
compute ind65 = 0.
compute ind66 = 0.
compute ind67 = 0.
compute ind68 = 0.
compute ind69 = 0.
compute ind70 = 0.
compute ind71 = 0.
compute ind72 = 0.
compute ind73 = 0.
compute ind74 = 0.
compute ind75 = 0.
compute ind76 = 0.
compute ind77 = 0.
compute ind78 = 0.
compute ind79 = 0.
compute ind80 = 0.
compute ind81 = 0.
compute ind82 = 0.
compute ind83 = 0.
compute ind84 = 0.
compute ind85 = 0.
compute ind86 = 0.
compute ind87 = 0.
compute ind88 = 0.
compute ind89 = 0.
compute ind90 = 0.
compute ind91 = 0.
compute ind92 = 0.
compute ind93 = 0.
compute ind94 = 0.
compute ind95 = 0.
compute ind96 = 0.
compute ind97 = 0.
compute ind98 = 0.
compute ind99 = 0.
do if (year < 2009).
if (kev_chan = 06)  ind00 = demand.
if (kev_chan = 07)  ind01 = demand.
if (kev_chan = 08)  ind02 = demand.
if (kev_chan = 09)  ind03 = demand.
if (kev_chan = 10)  ind04 = demand.
if (kev_chan = 11)  ind05 = demand.
if (kev_chan = 12)  ind06 = demand.
if (kev_mrch = 01)  ind11 = demand.
if (kev_mrch = 02)  ind11 = demand.
if (kev_mrch = 03)  ind12 = demand.
if (kev_mrch = 04)  ind13 = demand.
if (kev_mrch = 05)  ind13 = demand.
if (kev_mrch = 06)  ind14 = demand.
if (kev_mrch = 07)  ind15 = demand.
if (kev_mrch = 08)  ind15 = demand.
if (kev_mrch = 09)  ind15 = demand.
```

```
if (kev_mrch = 10)    ind15 = demand.
if (kev_mrch = 11)    ind11 = demand.
compute               ind21 = demand.
compute               ind22 = gross_margin.
end if.
compute recency = 999.
if (ord_date gt 20081100) and (ord_date le 20081200)  recency = 001.
if (ord_date gt 20081000) and (ord_date le 20081100)  recency = 002.
if (ord_date gt 20080900) and (ord_date le 20081000)  recency = 003.
if (ord_date gt 20080800) and (ord_date le 20080900)  recency = 004.
if (ord_date gt 20080700) and (ord_date le 20080800)  recency = 005.
if (ord_date gt 20080600) and (ord_date le 20080700)  recency = 006.
if (ord_date gt 20080500) and (ord_date le 20080600)  recency = 007.
if (ord_date gt 20080400) and (ord_date le 20080500)  recency = 008.
if (ord_date gt 20080300) and (ord_date le 20080400)  recency = 009.
if (ord_date gt 20080200) and (ord_date le 20080300)  recency = 010.
if (ord_date gt 20080100) and (ord_date le 20080200)  recency = 011.
if (ord_date gt 20071200) and (ord_date le 20080100)  recency = 012.
if (ord_date gt 20071100) and (ord_date le 20071200)  recency = 013.
if (ord_date gt 20071000) and (ord_date le 20071100)  recency = 014.
if (ord_date gt 20070900) and (ord_date le 20071000)  recency = 015.
if (ord_date gt 20070800) and (ord_date le 20070900)  recency = 016.
if (ord_date gt 20070700) and (ord_date le 20070800)  recency = 017.
if (ord_date gt 20070600) and (ord_date le 20070700)  recency = 018.
if (ord_date gt 20070500) and (ord_date le 20070600)  recency = 019.
if (ord_date gt 20070400) and (ord_date le 20070500)  recency = 020.
if (ord_date gt 20070300) and (ord_date le 20070400)  recency = 021.
if (ord_date gt 20070200) and (ord_date le 20070300)  recency = 022.
if (ord_date gt 20070100) and (ord_date le 20070200)  recency = 023.
if (ord_date gt 20061200) and (ord_date le 20070100)  recency = 024.
if (ord_date gt 20061100) and (ord_date le 20061200)  recency = 025.
if (ord_date gt 20061000) and (ord_date le 20061100)  recency = 026.
if (ord_date gt 20060900) and (ord_date le 20061000)  recency = 027.
if (ord_date gt 20060800) and (ord_date le 20060900)  recency = 028.
if (ord_date gt 20060700) and (ord_date le 20060800)  recency = 029.
if (ord_date gt 20060600) and (ord_date le 20060700)  recency = 030.
if (ord_date gt 20060500) and (ord_date le 20060600)  recency = 031.
if (ord_date gt 20060400) and (ord_date le 20060500)  recency = 032.
if (ord_date gt 20060300) and (ord_date le 20060400)  recency = 033.
if (ord_date gt 20060200) and (ord_date le 20060300)  recency = 034.
if (ord_date gt 20060100) and (ord_date le 20060200)  recency = 035.
if (ord_date gt 20051200) and (ord_date le 20060100)  recency = 036.
if (ord_date gt 20051100) and (ord_date le 20051200)  recency = 037.
if (ord_date gt 20051000) and (ord_date le 20051100)  recency = 038.
if (ord_date gt 20050900) and (ord_date le 20051000)  recency = 039.
if (ord_date gt 20050800) and (ord_date le 20050900)  recency = 040.
if (ord_date gt 20050700) and (ord_date le 20050800)  recency = 041.
if (ord_date gt 20050600) and (ord_date le 20050700)  recency = 042.
if (ord_date gt 20050500) and (ord_date le 20050600)  recency = 043.
if (ord_date gt 20050400) and (ord_date le 20050500)  recency = 044.
if (ord_date gt 20050300) and (ord_date le 20050400)  recency = 045.
if (ord_date gt 20050200) and (ord_date le 20050300)  recency = 046.
if (ord_date gt 20050100) and (ord_date le 20050200)  recency = 047.
if (ord_date gt 20041200) and (ord_date le 20050100)  recency = 048.
if (ord_date gt 20041100) and (ord_date le 20041200)  recency = 049.
if (ord_date gt 20041000) and (ord_date le 20041100)  recency = 050.
if (ord_date gt 20040900) and (ord_date le 20041000)  recency = 051.
if (ord_date gt 20040800) and (ord_date le 20040900)  recency = 052.
if (ord_date gt 20040700) and (ord_date le 20040800)  recency = 053.
if (ord_date gt 20040600) and (ord_date le 20040700)  recency = 054.
if (ord_date gt 20040500) and (ord_date le 20040600)  recency = 055.
if (ord_date gt 20040400) and (ord_date le 20040500)  recency = 056.
if (ord_date gt 20040300) and (ord_date le 20040400)  recency = 057.
if (ord_date gt 20040200) and (ord_date le 20040300)  recency = 058.
if (ord_date gt 20040100) and (ord_date le 20040200)  recency = 059.
if (ord_date gt 20031200) and (ord_date le 20040100)  recency = 060.
aggregate outfile = *
```

114

```
        /presorted
        /break            = household_id ord_date
        /rebuy            = max(rebuy)
        /future           = sum(future)
        /recency          = min(recency)
        /demd12 demd99    = sum(demd12 demd99)
        /freq12 freq99    = max(freq12 freq99)
        /item12 item99    = sum(item12 item99)
        /ind00 ind01 ind02 ind03 ind04 ind05 ind06 ind07 ind08 ind09
         ind10 ind11 ind12 ind13 ind14 ind15 ind16 ind17 ind18 ind19
         ind20 ind21 ind22 ind23 ind24 ind25 ind26 ind27 ind28 ind29
         ind30 ind31 ind32 ind33 ind34 ind35 ind36 ind37 ind38 ind39
         ind40 ind41 ind42 ind43 ind44 ind45 ind46 ind47 ind48 ind49
         ind50 ind51 ind52 ind53 ind54 ind55 ind56 ind57 ind58 ind59
         ind60 ind61 ind62 ind63 ind64 ind65 ind66 ind67 ind68 ind69
         ind70 ind71 ind72 ind73 ind74 ind75 ind76 ind77 ind78 ind79
         ind80 ind81 ind82 ind83 ind84 ind85 ind86 ind87 ind88 ind89
         ind90 ind91 ind92 ind93 ind94 ind95 ind96 ind97 ind98 ind99 = sum
        (ind00 ind01 ind02 ind03 ind04 ind05 ind06 ind07 ind08 ind09
         ind10 ind11 ind12 ind13 ind14 ind15 ind16 ind17 ind18 ind19
         ind20 ind21 ind22 ind23 ind24 ind25 ind26 ind27 ind28 ind29
         ind30 ind31 ind32 ind33 ind34 ind35 ind36 ind37 ind38 ind39
         ind40 ind41 ind42 ind43 ind44 ind45 ind46 ind47 ind48 ind49
         ind50 ind51 ind52 ind53 ind54 ind55 ind56 ind57 ind58 ind59
         ind60 ind61 ind62 ind63 ind64 ind65 ind66 ind67 ind68 ind69
         ind70 ind71 ind72 ind73 ind74 ind75 ind76 ind77 ind78 ind79
         ind80 ind81 ind82 ind83 ind84 ind85 ind86 ind87 ind88 ind89
         ind90 ind91 ind92 ind93 ind94 ind95 ind96 ind97 ind98 ind99).
aggregate outfile = *
        /presorted
        /break            = household_id
        /rebuy            = max(rebuy)
        /future           = sum(future)
        /recency          = min(recency)
        /demd12 demd99    = sum(demd12 demd99)
        /freq12 freq99    = sum(freq12 freq99)
        /item12 item99    = sum(item12 item99)
        /ind00 ind01 ind02 ind03 ind04 ind05 ind06 ind07 ind08 ind09
         ind10 ind11 ind12 ind13 ind14 ind15 ind16 ind17 ind18 ind19
         ind20 ind21 ind22 ind23 ind24 ind25 ind26 ind27 ind28 ind29
         ind30 ind31 ind32 ind33 ind34 ind35 ind36 ind37 ind38 ind39
         ind40 ind41 ind42 ind43 ind44 ind45 ind46 ind47 ind48 ind49
         ind50 ind51 ind52 ind53 ind54 ind55 ind56 ind57 ind58 ind59
         ind60 ind61 ind62 ind63 ind64 ind65 ind66 ind67 ind68 ind69
         ind70 ind71 ind72 ind73 ind74 ind75 ind76 ind77 ind78 ind79
         ind80 ind81 ind82 ind83 ind84 ind85 ind86 ind87 ind88 ind89
         ind90 ind91 ind92 ind93 ind94 ind95 ind96 ind97 ind98 ind99 = sum
        (ind00 ind01 ind02 ind03 ind04 ind05 ind06 ind07 ind08 ind09
         ind10 ind11 ind12 ind13 ind14 ind15 ind16 ind17 ind18 ind19
         ind20 ind21 ind22 ind23 ind24 ind25 ind26 ind27 ind28 ind29
         ind30 ind31 ind32 ind33 ind34 ind35 ind36 ind37 ind38 ind39
         ind40 ind41 ind42 ind43 ind44 ind45 ind46 ind47 ind48 ind49
         ind50 ind51 ind52 ind53 ind54 ind55 ind56 ind57 ind58 ind59
         ind60 ind61 ind62 ind63 ind64 ind65 ind66 ind67 ind68 ind69
         ind70 ind71 ind72 ind73 ind74 ind75 ind76 ind77 ind78 ind79
         ind80 ind81 ind82 ind83 ind84 ind85 ind86 ind87 ind88 ind89
         ind90 ind91 ind92 ind93 ind94 ind95 ind96 ind97 ind98 ind99).
select if recency ne 999.
compute root_rec = sqrt(recency).
formats rebuy(f1.0) recency(f3.0) freq12 to freq99(f3.0) item12 to
item99(f3.0).
save outfile = 'c:\datasets\OMS0.sav'.
execute.


*** Prepare The Datasets *** This Dataset Is For Reporting Purposes ***.
get file = 'c:\datasets\OMS_Book.sav'.
```

115

```
select if demand gt 0.
select if quantity gt 0.
select if (year = 2008).
compute demd12 = demand.
compute freq12 = 1.
compute item12 = quantity.
compute ind00 = 0.
compute ind01 = 0.
compute ind02 = 0.
compute ind03 = 0.
compute ind04 = 0.
compute ind05 = 0.
compute ind06 = 0.
compute ind07 = 0.
compute ind08 = 0.
compute ind09 = 0.
compute ind10 = 0.
compute ind11 = 0.
compute ind12 = 0.
compute ind13 = 0.
compute ind14 = 0.
compute ind15 = 0.
compute ind16 = 0.
compute ind17 = 0.
compute ind18 = 0.
compute ind19 = 0.
compute ind20 = 0.
compute ind21 = 0.
compute ind22 = 0.
compute ind23 = 0.
compute ind24 = 0.
compute ind25 = 0.
compute ind26 = 0.
compute ind27 = 0.
compute ind28 = 0.
compute ind29 = 0.
compute ind30 = 0.
compute ind31 = 0.
compute ind32 = 0.
compute ind33 = 0.
compute ind34 = 0.
compute ind35 = 0.
compute ind36 = 0.
compute ind37 = 0.
compute ind38 = 0.
compute ind39 = 0.
compute ind40 = 0.
compute ind41 = 0.
compute ind42 = 0.
compute ind43 = 0.
compute ind44 = 0.
compute ind45 = 0.
compute ind46 = 0.
compute ind47 = 0.
compute ind48 = 0.
compute ind49 = 0.
compute ind50 = 0.
compute ind51 = 0.
compute ind52 = 0.
compute ind53 = 0.
compute ind54 = 0.
compute ind55 = 0.
compute ind56 = 0.
compute ind57 = 0.
compute ind58 = 0.
compute ind59 = 0.
compute ind60 = 0.
```

```
compute ind61 = 0.
compute ind62 = 0.
compute ind63 = 0.
compute ind64 = 0.
compute ind65 = 0.
compute ind66 = 0.
compute ind67 = 0.
compute ind68 = 0.
compute ind69 = 0.
compute ind70 = 0.
compute ind71 = 0.
compute ind72 = 0.
compute ind73 = 0.
compute ind74 = 0.
compute ind75 = 0.
compute ind76 = 0.
compute ind77 = 0.
compute ind78 = 0.
compute ind79 = 0.
compute ind80 = 0.
compute ind81 = 0.
compute ind82 = 0.
compute ind83 = 0.
compute ind84 = 0.
compute ind85 = 0.
compute ind86 = 0.
compute ind87 = 0.
compute ind88 = 0.
compute ind89 = 0.
compute ind90 = 0.
compute ind91 = 0.
compute ind92 = 0.
compute ind93 = 0.
compute ind94 = 0.
compute ind95 = 0.
compute ind96 = 0.
compute ind97 = 0.
compute ind98 = 0.
compute ind99 = 0.
do if (year = 2008).
if (kev_chan = 06)  ind00 = demand.
if (kev_chan = 07)  ind01 = demand.
if (kev_chan = 08)  ind02 = demand.
if (kev_chan = 09)  ind03 = demand.
if (kev_chan = 10)  ind04 = demand.
if (kev_chan = 11)  ind05 = demand.
if (kev_chan = 12)  ind06 = demand.
if (kev_mrch = 01)  ind07 = demand.
if (kev_mrch = 02)  ind07 = demand.
if (kev_mrch = 03)  ind08 = demand.
if (kev_mrch = 04)  ind09 = demand.
if (kev_mrch = 05)  ind09 = demand.
if (kev_mrch = 06)  ind10 = demand.
if (kev_mrch = 07)  ind11 = demand.
if (kev_mrch = 08)  ind11 = demand.
if (kev_mrch = 09)  ind11 = demand.
if (kev_mrch = 10)  ind11 = demand.
if (kev_mrch = 11)  ind07 = demand.
compute             ind12 = demand.
compute             ind13 = gross_margin.
end if.
aggregate outfile = *
        /presorted
        /break          = household_id ord_date
        /demd12         = sum(demd12)
        /freq12         = max(freq12)
        /item12         = sum(item12)
```

117

```
        /ind00 ind01 ind02 ind03 ind04 ind05 ind06 ind07 ind08 ind09
         ind10 ind11 ind12 ind13 ind14 ind15 ind16 ind17 ind18 ind19
         ind20 ind21 ind22 ind23 ind24 ind25 ind26 ind27 ind28 ind29
         ind30 ind31 ind32 ind33 ind34 ind35 ind36 ind37 ind38 ind39
         ind40 ind41 ind42 ind43 ind44 ind45 ind46 ind47 ind48 ind49
         ind50 ind51 ind52 ind53 ind54 ind55 ind56 ind57 ind58 ind59
         ind60 ind61 ind62 ind63 ind64 ind65 ind66 ind67 ind68 ind69
         ind70 ind71 ind72 ind73 ind74 ind75 ind76 ind77 ind78 ind79
         ind80 ind81 ind82 ind83 ind84 ind85 ind86 ind87 ind88 ind89
         ind90 ind91 ind92 ind93 ind94 ind95 ind96 ind97 ind98 ind99 = sum
        (ind00 ind01 ind02 ind03 ind04 ind05 ind06 ind07 ind08 ind09
         ind10 ind11 ind12 ind13 ind14 ind15 ind16 ind17 ind18 ind19
         ind20 ind21 ind22 ind23 ind24 ind25 ind26 ind27 ind28 ind29
         ind30 ind31 ind32 ind33 ind34 ind35 ind36 ind37 ind38 ind39
         ind40 ind41 ind42 ind43 ind44 ind45 ind46 ind47 ind48 ind49
         ind50 ind51 ind52 ind53 ind54 ind55 ind56 ind57 ind58 ind59
         ind60 ind61 ind62 ind63 ind64 ind65 ind66 ind67 ind68 ind69
         ind70 ind71 ind72 ind73 ind74 ind75 ind76 ind77 ind78 ind79
         ind80 ind81 ind82 ind83 ind84 ind85 ind86 ind87 ind88 ind89
         ind90 ind91 ind92 ind93 ind94 ind95 ind96 ind97 ind98 ind99).
aggregate outfile = *
        /presorted
        /break          = household_id
        /demd12         = sum(demd12)
        /freq12         = sum(freq12)
        /item12         = sum(item12)
        /ind00 ind01 ind02 ind03 ind04 ind05 ind06 ind07 ind08 ind09
         ind10 ind11 ind12 ind13 ind14 ind15 ind16 ind17 ind18 ind19
         ind20 ind21 ind22 ind23 ind24 ind25 ind26 ind27 ind28 ind29
         ind30 ind31 ind32 ind33 ind34 ind35 ind36 ind37 ind38 ind39
         ind40 ind41 ind42 ind43 ind44 ind45 ind46 ind47 ind48 ind49
         ind50 ind51 ind52 ind53 ind54 ind55 ind56 ind57 ind58 ind59
         ind60 ind61 ind62 ind63 ind64 ind65 ind66 ind67 ind68 ind69
         ind70 ind71 ind72 ind73 ind74 ind75 ind76 ind77 ind78 ind79
         ind80 ind81 ind82 ind83 ind84 ind85 ind86 ind87 ind88 ind89
         ind90 ind91 ind92 ind93 ind94 ind95 ind96 ind97 ind98 ind99 = sum
        (ind00 ind01 ind02 ind03 ind04 ind05 ind06 ind07 ind08 ind09
         ind10 ind11 ind12 ind13 ind14 ind15 ind16 ind17 ind18 ind19
         ind20 ind21 ind22 ind23 ind24 ind25 ind26 ind27 ind28 ind29
         ind30 ind31 ind32 ind33 ind34 ind35 ind36 ind37 ind38 ind39
         ind40 ind41 ind42 ind43 ind44 ind45 ind46 ind47 ind48 ind49
         ind50 ind51 ind52 ind53 ind54 ind55 ind56 ind57 ind58 ind59
         ind60 ind61 ind62 ind63 ind64 ind65 ind66 ind67 ind68 ind69
         ind70 ind71 ind72 ind73 ind74 ind75 ind76 ind77 ind78 ind79
         ind80 ind81 ind82 ind83 ind84 ind85 ind86 ind87 ind88 ind89
         ind90 ind91 ind92 ind93 ind94 ind95 ind96 ind97 ind98 ind99).
formats freq12(f3.0) item12(f3.0) ind00 to ind99(f1.0).
save outfile = 'c:\datasets\OMS2.sav'.
execute.



*** Run The Regression Models Here ***.
get file = 'c:\datasets\OMS1.sav'.
compute ind00 = ind00 / (demd12 + demd99).
compute ind01 = ind01 / (demd12 + demd99).
compute ind02 = ind02 / (demd12 + demd99).
compute ind03 = ind03 / (demd12 + demd99).
compute ind04 = ind04 / (demd12 + demd99).
compute ind05 = ind05 / (demd12 + demd99).
compute ind06 = ind06 / (demd12 + demd99).
compute ind07 = ind07 / (demd12 + demd99).
compute ind08 = ind08 / (demd12 + demd99).
compute ind09 = ind09 / (demd12 + demd99).
compute ind10 = ind10 / (demd12 + demd99).
compute ind11 = ind11 / (demd12 + demd99).
compute ind12 = ind12 / (demd12 + demd99).
```

118

```
compute ind13 = ind13 / (demd12 + demd99).
compute ind14 = ind14 / (demd12 + demd99).
compute ind15 = ind15 / (demd12 + demd99).
compute ind16 = ind16 / (demd12 + demd99).
compute ind17 = ind17 / (demd12 + demd99).
compute ind18 = ind18 / (demd12 + demd99).
compute ind19 = ind19 / (demd12 + demd99).
compute ind20 = ind20 / (demd12 + demd99).
compute ind21 = ind21 / (demd12 + demd99).
compute ind22 = ind22 / (demd12 + demd99).
compute ind23 = ind23 / (demd12 + demd99).
compute ind24 = ind24 / (demd12 + demd99).
compute ind25 = ind25 / (demd12 + demd99).
compute ind26 = ind26 / (demd12 + demd99).
compute ind27 = ind27 / (demd12 + demd99).
compute ind28 = ind28 / (demd12 + demd99).
compute ind29 = ind29 / (demd12 + demd99).
compute ind30 = ind30 / (demd12 + demd99).
compute ind31 = ind31 / (demd12 + demd99).
compute ind32 = ind32 / (demd12 + demd99).
compute ind33 = ind33 / (demd12 + demd99).
compute ind34 = ind34 / (demd12 + demd99).
compute ind35 = ind35 / (demd12 + demd99).
compute ind36 = ind36 / (demd12 + demd99).
compute ind37 = ind37 / (demd12 + demd99).
compute ind38 = ind38 / (demd12 + demd99).
compute ind39 = ind39 / (demd12 + demd99).
compute ind40 = ind40 / (demd12 + demd99).
compute ind41 = ind41 / (demd12 + demd99).
compute ind42 = ind42 / (demd12 + demd99).
compute ind43 = ind43 / (demd12 + demd99).
compute ind44 = ind44 / (demd12 + demd99).
compute ind45 = ind45 / (demd12 + demd99).
compute ind46 = ind46 / (demd12 + demd99).
compute ind47 = ind47 / (demd12 + demd99).
compute ind48 = ind48 / (demd12 + demd99).
compute ind49 = ind49 / (demd12 + demd99).
*** A Very Simple Regression Model ***.
LOGISTIC REGRESSION VARIABLES  rebuy
  /METHOD = ENTER root_rec freq12 freq99
  /CRITERIA = PIN(.05) POUT(.10) ITERATE(500) CUT(.5).
compute spend = $sysmis.
if (rebuy = 1)  spend = future.
REGRESSION
  /MISSING LISTWISE
  /STATISTICS COEFF OUTS R ANOVA
  /CRITERIA=PIN(.05) POUT(.10)
  /NOORIGIN
  /DEPENDENT spend
  /METHOD=ENTER demd12 demd99.
execute.


*** Score Last Years File Here ***.
get file = 'c:\datasets\OMS1.sav'.
compute ind00 = ind00 / (demd12 + demd99).
compute ind01 = ind01 / (demd12 + demd99).
compute ind02 = ind02 / (demd12 + demd99).
compute ind03 = ind03 / (demd12 + demd99).
compute ind04 = ind04 / (demd12 + demd99).
compute ind05 = ind05 / (demd12 + demd99).
compute ind06 = ind06 / (demd12 + demd99).
compute ind07 = ind07 / (demd12 + demd99).
compute ind08 = ind08 / (demd12 + demd99).
compute ind09 = ind09 / (demd12 + demd99).
compute ind10 = ind10 / (demd12 + demd99).
compute ind11 = ind11 / (demd12 + demd99).
```

119

```
compute ind12 = ind12 / (demd12 + demd99).
compute ind13 = ind13 / (demd12 + demd99).
compute ind14 = ind14 / (demd12 + demd99).
compute ind15 = ind15 / (demd12 + demd99).
compute ind16 = ind16 / (demd12 + demd99).
compute ind17 = ind17 / (demd12 + demd99).
compute ind18 = ind18 / (demd12 + demd99).
compute ind19 = ind19 / (demd12 + demd99).
compute ind20 = ind20 / (demd12 + demd99).
compute ind21 = ind21 / (demd12 + demd99).
compute ind22 = ind22 / (demd12 + demd99).
compute ind23 = ind23 / (demd12 + demd99).
compute ind24 = ind24 / (demd12 + demd99).
compute ind25 = ind25 / (demd12 + demd99).
compute ind26 = ind26 / (demd12 + demd99).
compute ind27 = ind27 / (demd12 + demd99).
compute ind28 = ind28 / (demd12 + demd99).
compute ind29 = ind29 / (demd12 + demd99).
compute ind30 = ind30 / (demd12 + demd99).
compute ind31 = ind31 / (demd12 + demd99).
compute ind32 = ind32 / (demd12 + demd99).
compute ind33 = ind33 / (demd12 + demd99).
compute ind34 = ind34 / (demd12 + demd99).
compute ind35 = ind35 / (demd12 + demd99).
compute ind36 = ind36 / (demd12 + demd99).
compute ind37 = ind37 / (demd12 + demd99).
compute ind38 = ind38 / (demd12 + demd99).
compute ind39 = ind39 / (demd12 + demd99).
compute ind40 = ind40 / (demd12 + demd99).
compute ind41 = ind41 / (demd12 + demd99).
compute ind42 = ind42 / (demd12 + demd99).
compute ind43 = ind43 / (demd12 + demd99).
compute ind44 = ind44 / (demd12 + demd99).
compute ind45 = ind45 / (demd12 + demd99).
compute ind46 = ind46 / (demd12 + demd99).
compute ind47 = ind47 / (demd12 + demd99).
compute ind48 = ind48 / (demd12 + demd99).
compute ind49 = ind49 / (demd12 + demd99).
compute predr = -0.893 - 0.363*root_rec + 0.460*freq12 + 0.153*freq99.
compute predr = EXP(predr) / (1 + EXP(predr)).
compute preds = 181.857 + 0.377*demd12 + 0.066*demd99.
compute predv = predr * preds.
FREQUENCIES
  VARIABLES=predv
  /FORMAT=NOTABLE
  /NTILES= 20
  /ORDER=  ANALYSIS.
execute.
*** Make Adjustments For Segmentation ***.
compute f1 = 7.
compute f2 = 6.
if (ind00 > 0.550)  f1 = 0.
if (ind01 > 0.550)  f1 = 1.
if (ind02 > 0.550)  f1 = 2.
if (ind03 > 0.550)  f1 = 3.
if (ind04 > 0.550)  f1 = 4.
if (ind05 > 0.550)  f1 = 5.
if (ind06 > 0.550)  f1 = 6.
if (ind11 > 0.550)  f2 = 1.
if (ind12 > 0.550)  f2 = 2.
if (ind13 > 0.550)  f2 = 3.
if (ind14 > 0.550)  f2 = 4.
if (ind15 > 0.550)  f2 = 5.
string s0(a1).
string s1(a1).
string s2(a1).
string s3(a1).
```

```
string s4(a1).
string s5(a1).
if (predv ge 100.3)                         s0 = 'A'.
if (predv ge  41.2) and (predv lt 100.3)    s0 = 'B'.
if (predv ge  17.5) and (predv lt  41.2)    s0 = 'C'.
if (predv ge   9.8) and (predv lt  17.5)    s0 = 'D'.
if (predv ge   0.0) and (predv lt   9.8)    s0 = 'F'.
compute s1 = 'H'.
if (f1 = 0)   s1 = 'A'.
if (f1 = 1)   s1 = 'B'.
if (f1 = 2)   s1 = 'C'.
if (f1 = 3)   s1 = 'D'.
if (f1 = 4)   s1 = 'E'.
if (f1 = 5)   s1 = 'F'.
if (f1 = 6)   s1 = 'G'.
compute s2 = 'F'.
if (f2 = 1)   s2 = 'A'.
if (f2 = 2)   s2 = 'B'.
if (f2 = 3)   s2 = 'C'.
if (f2 = 4)   s2 = 'D'.
if (f2 = 5)   s2 = 'E'.
string gradep(a6).
compute gradep = concat(s0,s1,s2).
frequencies variables = gradep s0 s1 s2.
save outfile = 'c:\datasets\OMS4.sav'
        /keep = household_id gradep.
execute.


*** Score Next Years File Here ***.
get file = 'c:\datasets\OMS0.sav'.
*** Plug In Code From Above Right Here *****.
compute ind00 = ind00 / (demd12 + demd99).
compute ind01 = ind01 / (demd12 + demd99).
compute ind02 = ind02 / (demd12 + demd99).
compute ind03 = ind03 / (demd12 + demd99).
compute ind04 = ind04 / (demd12 + demd99).
compute ind05 = ind05 / (demd12 + demd99).
compute ind06 = ind06 / (demd12 + demd99).
compute ind07 = ind07 / (demd12 + demd99).
compute ind08 = ind08 / (demd12 + demd99).
compute ind09 = ind09 / (demd12 + demd99).
compute ind10 = ind10 / (demd12 + demd99).
compute ind11 = ind11 / (demd12 + demd99).
compute ind12 = ind12 / (demd12 + demd99).
compute ind13 = ind13 / (demd12 + demd99).
compute ind14 = ind14 / (demd12 + demd99).
compute ind15 = ind15 / (demd12 + demd99).
compute ind16 = ind16 / (demd12 + demd99).
compute ind17 = ind17 / (demd12 + demd99).
compute ind18 = ind18 / (demd12 + demd99).
compute ind19 = ind19 / (demd12 + demd99).
compute ind20 = ind20 / (demd12 + demd99).
compute ind21 = ind21 / (demd12 + demd99).
compute ind22 = ind22 / (demd12 + demd99).
compute ind23 = ind23 / (demd12 + demd99).
compute ind24 = ind24 / (demd12 + demd99).
compute ind25 = ind25 / (demd12 + demd99).
compute ind26 = ind26 / (demd12 + demd99).
compute ind27 = ind27 / (demd12 + demd99).
compute ind28 = ind28 / (demd12 + demd99).
compute ind29 = ind29 / (demd12 + demd99).
compute ind30 = ind30 / (demd12 + demd99).
compute ind31 = ind31 / (demd12 + demd99).
compute ind32 = ind32 / (demd12 + demd99).
compute ind33 = ind33 / (demd12 + demd99).
compute ind34 = ind34 / (demd12 + demd99).
```

```
compute ind35 = ind35 / (demd12 + demd99).
compute ind36 = ind36 / (demd12 + demd99).
compute ind37 = ind37 / (demd12 + demd99).
compute ind38 = ind38 / (demd12 + demd99).
compute ind39 = ind39 / (demd12 + demd99).
compute ind40 = ind40 / (demd12 + demd99).
compute ind41 = ind41 / (demd12 + demd99).
compute ind42 = ind42 / (demd12 + demd99).
compute ind43 = ind43 / (demd12 + demd99).
compute ind44 = ind44 / (demd12 + demd99).
compute ind45 = ind45 / (demd12 + demd99).
compute ind46 = ind46 / (demd12 + demd99).
compute ind47 = ind47 / (demd12 + demd99).
compute ind48 = ind48 / (demd12 + demd99).
compute ind49 = ind49 / (demd12 + demd99).
compute predr = -0.893 - 0.363*root_rec + 0.460*freq12 + 0.153*freq99.
compute predr = EXP(predr) / (1 + EXP(predr)).
compute preds = 181.857 + 0.377*demd12 + 0.066*demd99.
compute predv = predr * preds.
FREQUENCIES
  VARIABLES=predv
  /FORMAT=NOTABLE
  /NTILES= 20
  /ORDER=  ANALYSIS.
execute.
*** Make Adjustments For Segmentation ***.
compute f1 = 7.
compute f2 = 6.
if (ind00 > 0.550)   f1 = 0.
if (ind01 > 0.550)   f1 = 1.
if (ind02 > 0.550)   f1 = 2.
if (ind03 > 0.550)   f1 = 3.
if (ind04 > 0.550)   f1 = 4.
if (ind05 > 0.550)   f1 = 5.
if (ind06 > 0.550)   f1 = 6.
if (ind11 > 0.550)   f2 = 1.
if (ind12 > 0.550)   f2 = 2.
if (ind13 > 0.550)   f2 = 3.
if (ind14 > 0.550)   f2 = 4.
if (ind15 > 0.550)   f2 = 5.
string s0(a1).
string s1(a1).
string s2(a1).
string s3(a1).
string s4(a1).
string s5(a1).
if (predv ge 100.3)                        s0 = 'A'.
if (predv ge   41.2) and (predv lt 100.3)  s0 = 'B'.
if (predv ge   17.5) and (predv lt  41.2)  s0 = 'C'.
if (predv ge    9.8) and (predv lt  17.5)  s0 = 'D'.
if (predv ge    0.0) and (predv lt   9.8)  s0 = 'F'.
compute s1 = 'H'.
if (f1 = 0)   s1 = 'A'.
if (f1 = 1)   s1 = 'B'.
if (f1 = 2)   s1 = 'C'.
if (f1 = 3)   s1 = 'D'.
if (f1 = 4)   s1 = 'E'.
if (f1 = 5)   s1 = 'F'.
if (f1 = 6)   s1 = 'G'.
compute s2 = 'F'.
if (f2 = 1)   s2 = 'A'.
if (f2 = 2)   s2 = 'B'.
if (f2 = 3)   s2 = 'C'.
if (f2 = 4)   s2 = 'D'.
if (f2 = 5)   s2 = 'E'.
string gradef(a6).
compute gradef = concat(s0,s1,s2).
```

```
frequencies variables = gradef s0 s1 s2.
save outfile = 'c:\datasets\OMS5.sav'
            /keep = household_id gradef.
execute.


*** Match Up All Relevant Datasets Here ***.
match files  file = 'c:\datasets\OMS4.sav'
            /file = 'c:\datasets\OMS5.sav'
              /by = household_id.
match files  file = *
            /file = 'c:\datasets\OMS2.sav'
              /by = household_id.
do if missing(ind01).
compute demd12 = 0.
compute freq12 = 0.
compute item12 = 0.
compute ind00 = 0.
compute ind01 = 0.
compute ind02 = 0.
compute ind03 = 0.
compute ind04 = 0.
compute ind05 = 0.
compute ind06 = 0.
compute ind07 = 0.
compute ind08 = 0.
compute ind09 = 0.
compute ind10 = 0.
compute ind11 = 0.
compute ind12 = 0.
compute ind13 = 0.
compute ind14 = 0.
compute ind15 = 0.
compute ind16 = 0.
compute ind17 = 0.
compute ind18 = 0.
compute ind19 = 0.
compute ind20 = 0.
compute ind21 = 0.
compute ind22 = 0.
compute ind23 = 0.
compute ind24 = 0.
compute ind25 = 0.
compute ind26 = 0.
compute ind27 = 0.
compute ind28 = 0.
compute ind29 = 0.
compute ind30 = 0.
compute ind31 = 0.
compute ind32 = 0.
compute ind33 = 0.
compute ind34 = 0.
compute ind35 = 0.
compute ind36 = 0.
compute ind37 = 0.
compute ind38 = 0.
compute ind39 = 0.
compute ind40 = 0.
compute ind41 = 0.
compute ind42 = 0.
compute ind43 = 0.
compute ind44 = 0.
compute ind45 = 0.
compute ind46 = 0.
compute ind47 = 0.
compute ind48 = 0.
compute ind49 = 0.
```

123

```
compute ind50 = 0.
compute ind51 = 0.
compute ind52 = 0.
compute ind53 = 0.
compute ind54 = 0.
compute ind55 = 0.
compute ind56 = 0.
compute ind57 = 0.
compute ind58 = 0.
compute ind59 = 0.
compute ind60 = 0.
compute ind61 = 0.
compute ind62 = 0.
compute ind63 = 0.
compute ind64 = 0.
compute ind65 = 0.
compute ind66 = 0.
compute ind67 = 0.
compute ind68 = 0.
compute ind69 = 0.
compute ind70 = 0.
compute ind71 = 0.
compute ind72 = 0.
compute ind73 = 0.
compute ind74 = 0.
compute ind75 = 0.
compute ind76 = 0.
compute ind77 = 0.
compute ind78 = 0.
compute ind79 = 0.
compute ind80 = 0.
compute ind81 = 0.
compute ind82 = 0.
compute ind83 = 0.
compute ind84 = 0.
compute ind85 = 0.
compute ind86 = 0.
compute ind87 = 0.
compute ind88 = 0.
compute ind89 = 0.
compute ind90 = 0.
compute ind91 = 0.
compute ind92 = 0.
compute ind93 = 0.
compute ind94 = 0.
compute ind95 = 0.
compute ind96 = 0.
compute ind97 = 0.
compute ind98 = 0.
compute ind99 = 0.
end if.
compute buyr12 = 0.
if (demd12 > 0)  buyr12 = 1.
compute newb12 = 0.
if (gradep = ' ')  newb12 = 1.
if (gradep = ' ')  gradep = 'ZZZZZZ'.
save outfile = 'c:\datasets\OMS6.sav'
        /keep = household_id gradep gradef buyr12 newb12 demd12 freq12
item12 ind00 to ind99.
execute.


*** Audit For Segments With No Prior Year Activity But Does Have Future Year
Activity ***.
get file = 'c:\datasets\OMS6.sav'.
aggregate outfile = *
        /break           = gradep
```

124

```
        /casesly          = n.
string grade(a6).
compute grade = gradep.
formats casesly(f8.0).
save outfile = 'c:\datasets\dummy.sav'.
execute.
get file = 'c:\datasets\OMS6.sav'.
aggregate outfile = *
        /break            = gradef
        /casesny          = n.
string grade(a6).
compute grade = gradef.
formats casesny(f8.0).
match files  file = 'c:\datasets\dummy.sav'
            /file = *
            /by = grade.
list variables = grade casesly casesny.
execute.


*** Create The 5x8x6 = 240 Possible Segments ***.
get file = 'c:\datasets\OMS6.sav'.
compute rebuy = 0.
if (buyr12 > 0)  rebuy = 1.
formats rebuy(f1.0).
*** Historical Segments First ***.
string seg(a6).
compute seg = gradep.
compute seg1 = 0.
if (seg = 'AAA')  seg1 = 001.
if (seg = 'AAB')  seg1 = 002.
if (seg = 'AAC')  seg1 = 003.
if (seg = 'AAD')  seg1 = 004.
if (seg = 'AAE')  seg1 = 005.
if (seg = 'AAF')  seg1 = 006.
if (seg = 'ABA')  seg1 = 007.
if (seg = 'ABB')  seg1 = 008.
if (seg = 'ABC')  seg1 = 009.
if (seg = 'ABD')  seg1 = 010.
if (seg = 'ABE')  seg1 = 011.
if (seg = 'ABF')  seg1 = 012.
if (seg = 'ACA')  seg1 = 013.
if (seg = 'ACB')  seg1 = 014.
if (seg = 'ACC')  seg1 = 015.
if (seg = 'ACD')  seg1 = 016.
if (seg = 'ACE')  seg1 = 017.
if (seg = 'ACF')  seg1 = 018.
if (seg = 'ADA')  seg1 = 019.
if (seg = 'ADB')  seg1 = 020.
if (seg = 'ADC')  seg1 = 021.
if (seg = 'ADD')  seg1 = 022.
if (seg = 'ADE')  seg1 = 023.
if (seg = 'ADF')  seg1 = 024.
if (seg = 'AEA')  seg1 = 025.
if (seg = 'AEB')  seg1 = 026.
if (seg = 'AEC')  seg1 = 027.
if (seg = 'AED')  seg1 = 028.
if (seg = 'AEE')  seg1 = 029.
if (seg = 'AEF')  seg1 = 030.
if (seg = 'AFA')  seg1 = 031.
if (seg = 'AFB')  seg1 = 032.
if (seg = 'AFC')  seg1 = 033.
if (seg = 'AFD')  seg1 = 034.
if (seg = 'AFE')  seg1 = 035.
if (seg = 'AFF')  seg1 = 036.
if (seg = 'AGA')  seg1 = 037.
```

```
if (seg = 'AGB')   seg1 = 038.
if (seg = 'AGC')   seg1 = 039.
if (seg = 'AGD')   seg1 = 040.
if (seg = 'AGE')   seg1 = 041.
if (seg = 'AGF')   seg1 = 042.
if (seg = 'AHA')   seg1 = 043.
if (seg = 'AHB')   seg1 = 044.
if (seg = 'AHC')   seg1 = 045.
if (seg = 'AHD')   seg1 = 046.
if (seg = 'AHE')   seg1 = 047.
if (seg = 'AHF')   seg1 = 048.
if (seg = 'BAA')   seg1 = 049.
if (seg = 'BAB')   seg1 = 050.
if (seg = 'BAC')   seg1 = 051.
if (seg = 'BAD')   seg1 = 052.
if (seg = 'BAE')   seg1 = 053.
if (seg = 'BAF')   seg1 = 054.
if (seg = 'BBA')   seg1 = 055.
if (seg = 'BBB')   seg1 = 056.
if (seg = 'BBC')   seg1 = 057.
if (seg = 'BBD')   seg1 = 058.
if (seg = 'BBE')   seg1 = 059.
if (seg = 'BBF')   seg1 = 060.
if (seg = 'BCA')   seg1 = 061.
if (seg = 'BCB')   seg1 = 062.
if (seg = 'BCC')   seg1 = 063.
if (seg = 'BCD')   seg1 = 064.
if (seg = 'BCE')   seg1 = 065.
if (seg = 'BCF')   seg1 = 066.
if (seg = 'BDA')   seg1 = 067.
if (seg = 'BDB')   seg1 = 068.
if (seg = 'BDC')   seg1 = 069.
if (seg = 'BDD')   seg1 = 070.
if (seg = 'BDE')   seg1 = 071.
if (seg = 'BDF')   seg1 = 072.
if (seg = 'BEA')   seg1 = 073.
if (seg = 'BEB')   seg1 = 074.
if (seg = 'BEC')   seg1 = 075.
if (seg = 'BED')   seg1 = 076.
if (seg = 'BEE')   seg1 = 077.
if (seg = 'BEF')   seg1 = 078.
if (seg = 'BFA')   seg1 = 079.
if (seg = 'BFB')   seg1 = 080.
if (seg = 'BFC')   seg1 = 081.
if (seg = 'BFD')   seg1 = 082.
if (seg = 'BFE')   seg1 = 083.
if (seg = 'BFF')   seg1 = 084.
if (seg = 'BGA')   seg1 = 085.
if (seg = 'BGB')   seg1 = 086.
if (seg = 'BGC')   seg1 = 087.
if (seg = 'BGD')   seg1 = 088.
if (seg = 'BGE')   seg1 = 089.
if (seg = 'BGF')   seg1 = 090.
if (seg = 'BHA')   seg1 = 091.
if (seg = 'BHB')   seg1 = 092.
if (seg = 'BHC')   seg1 = 093.
if (seg = 'BHD')   seg1 = 094.
if (seg = 'BHE')   seg1 = 095.
if (seg = 'BHF')   seg1 = 096.
if (seg = 'CAA')   seg1 = 097.
if (seg = 'CAB')   seg1 = 098.
if (seg = 'CAC')   seg1 = 099.
if (seg = 'CAD')   seg1 = 100.
if (seg = 'CAE')   seg1 = 101.
if (seg = 'CAF')   seg1 = 102.
if (seg = 'CBA')   seg1 = 103.
if (seg = 'CBB')   seg1 = 104.
```

```
if (seg = 'CBC')  seg1 = 105.
if (seg = 'CBD')  seg1 = 106.
if (seg = 'CBE')  seg1 = 107.
if (seg = 'CBF')  seg1 = 108.
if (seg = 'CCA')  seg1 = 109.
if (seg = 'CCB')  seg1 = 110.
if (seg = 'CCC')  seg1 = 111.
if (seg = 'CCD')  seg1 = 112.
if (seg = 'CCE')  seg1 = 113.
if (seg = 'CCF')  seg1 = 114.
if (seg = 'CDA')  seg1 = 115.
if (seg = 'CDB')  seg1 = 116.
if (seg = 'CDC')  seg1 = 117.
if (seg = 'CDD')  seg1 = 118.
if (seg = 'CDE')  seg1 = 119.
if (seg = 'CDF')  seg1 = 120.
if (seg = 'CEA')  seg1 = 121.
if (seg = 'CEB')  seg1 = 122.
if (seg = 'CEC')  seg1 = 123.
if (seg = 'CED')  seg1 = 124.
if (seg = 'CEE')  seg1 = 125.
if (seg = 'CEF')  seg1 = 126.
if (seg = 'CFA')  seg1 = 127.
if (seg = 'CFB')  seg1 = 128.
if (seg = 'CFC')  seg1 = 129.
if (seg = 'CFD')  seg1 = 130.
if (seg = 'CFE')  seg1 = 131.
if (seg = 'CFF')  seg1 = 132.
if (seg = 'CGA')  seg1 = 133.
if (seg = 'CGB')  seg1 = 134.
if (seg = 'CGC')  seg1 = 135.
if (seg = 'CGD')  seg1 = 136.
if (seg = 'CGE')  seg1 = 137.
if (seg = 'CGF')  seg1 = 138.
if (seg = 'CHA')  seg1 = 139.
if (seg = 'CHB')  seg1 = 140.
if (seg = 'CHC')  seg1 = 141.
if (seg = 'CHD')  seg1 = 142.
if (seg = 'CHE')  seg1 = 143.
if (seg = 'CHF')  seg1 = 144.
if (seg = 'DAA')  seg1 = 145.
if (seg = 'DAB')  seg1 = 146.
if (seg = 'DAC')  seg1 = 147.
if (seg = 'DAD')  seg1 = 148.
if (seg = 'DAE')  seg1 = 149.
if (seg = 'DAF')  seg1 = 150.
if (seg = 'DBA')  seg1 = 151.
if (seg = 'DBB')  seg1 = 152.
if (seg = 'DBC')  seg1 = 153.
if (seg = 'DBD')  seg1 = 154.
if (seg = 'DBE')  seg1 = 155.
if (seg = 'DBF')  seg1 = 156.
if (seg = 'DCA')  seg1 = 157.
if (seg = 'DCB')  seg1 = 158.
if (seg = 'DCC')  seg1 = 159.
if (seg = 'DCD')  seg1 = 160.
if (seg = 'DCE')  seg1 = 161.
if (seg = 'DCF')  seg1 = 162.
if (seg = 'DDA')  seg1 = 163.
if (seg = 'DDB')  seg1 = 164.
if (seg = 'DDC')  seg1 = 165.
if (seg = 'DDD')  seg1 = 166.
if (seg = 'DDE')  seg1 = 167.
if (seg = 'DDF')  seg1 = 168.
if (seg = 'DEA')  seg1 = 169.
if (seg = 'DEB')  seg1 = 170.
if (seg = 'DEC')  seg1 = 171.
```

```
if (seg = 'DED')   seg1 = 172.
if (seg = 'DEE')   seg1 = 173.
if (seg = 'DEF')   seg1 = 174.
if (seg = 'DFA')   seg1 = 175.
if (seg = 'DFB')   seg1 = 176.
if (seg = 'DFC')   seg1 = 177.
if (seg = 'DFD')   seg1 = 178.
if (seg = 'DFE')   seg1 = 179.
if (seg = 'DFF')   seg1 = 180.
if (seg = 'DGA')   seg1 = 181.
if (seg = 'DGB')   seg1 = 182.
if (seg = 'DGC')   seg1 = 183.
if (seg = 'DGD')   seg1 = 184.
if (seg = 'DGE')   seg1 = 185.
if (seg = 'DGF')   seg1 = 186.
if (seg = 'DHA')   seg1 = 187.
if (seg = 'DHB')   seg1 = 188.
if (seg = 'DHC')   seg1 = 189.
if (seg = 'DHD')   seg1 = 190.
if (seg = 'DHE')   seg1 = 191.
if (seg = 'DHF')   seg1 = 192.
if (seg = 'FAA')   seg1 = 193.
if (seg = 'FAB')   seg1 = 194.
if (seg = 'FAC')   seg1 = 195.
if (seg = 'FAD')   seg1 = 196.
if (seg = 'FAE')   seg1 = 197.
if (seg = 'FAF')   seg1 = 198.
if (seg = 'FBA')   seg1 = 199.
if (seg = 'FBB')   seg1 = 200.
if (seg = 'FBC')   seg1 = 201.
if (seg = 'FBD')   seg1 = 202.
if (seg = 'FBE')   seg1 = 203.
if (seg = 'FBF')   seg1 = 204.
if (seg = 'FCA')   seg1 = 205.
if (seg = 'FCB')   seg1 = 206.
if (seg = 'FCC')   seg1 = 207.
if (seg = 'FCD')   seg1 = 208.
if (seg = 'FCE')   seg1 = 209.
if (seg = 'FCF')   seg1 = 210.
if (seg = 'FDA')   seg1 = 211.
if (seg = 'FDB')   seg1 = 212.
if (seg = 'FDC')   seg1 = 213.
if (seg = 'FDD')   seg1 = 214.
if (seg = 'FDE')   seg1 = 215.
if (seg = 'FDF')   seg1 = 216.
if (seg = 'FEA')   seg1 = 217.
if (seg = 'FEB')   seg1 = 218.
if (seg = 'FEC')   seg1 = 219.
if (seg = 'FED')   seg1 = 220.
if (seg = 'FEE')   seg1 = 221.
if (seg = 'FEF')   seg1 = 222.
if (seg = 'FFA')   seg1 = 223.
if (seg = 'FFB')   seg1 = 224.
if (seg = 'FFC')   seg1 = 225.
if (seg = 'FFD')   seg1 = 226.
if (seg = 'FFE')   seg1 = 227.
if (seg = 'FFF')   seg1 = 228.
if (seg = 'FGA')   seg1 = 229.
if (seg = 'FGB')   seg1 = 230.
if (seg = 'FGC')   seg1 = 231.
if (seg = 'FGD')   seg1 = 232.
if (seg = 'FGE')   seg1 = 233.
if (seg = 'FGF')   seg1 = 234.
if (seg = 'FHA')   seg1 = 235.
if (seg = 'FHB')   seg1 = 236.
if (seg = 'FHC')   seg1 = 237.
if (seg = 'FHD')   seg1 = 238.
```

```
if (seg = 'FHE')    seg1 = 239.
if (seg = 'FHF')    seg1 = 240.
compute seg = gradef.
compute seg2 = 0.
if (seg = 'AAA')    seg2 = 001.
if (seg = 'AAB')    seg2 = 002.
if (seg = 'AAC')    seg2 = 003.
if (seg = 'AAD')    seg2 = 004.
if (seg = 'AAE')    seg2 = 005.
if (seg = 'AAF')    seg2 = 006.
if (seg = 'ABA')    seg2 = 007.
if (seg = 'ABB')    seg2 = 008.
if (seg = 'ABC')    seg2 = 009.
if (seg = 'ABD')    seg2 = 010.
if (seg = 'ABE')    seg2 = 011.
if (seg = 'ABF')    seg2 = 012.
if (seg = 'ACA')    seg2 = 013.
if (seg = 'ACB')    seg2 = 014.
if (seg = 'ACC')    seg2 = 015.
if (seg = 'ACD')    seg2 = 016.
if (seg = 'ACE')    seg2 = 017.
if (seg = 'ACF')    seg2 = 018.
if (seg = 'ADA')    seg2 = 019.
if (seg = 'ADB')    seg2 = 020.
if (seg = 'ADC')    seg2 = 021.
if (seg = 'ADD')    seg2 = 022.
if (seg = 'ADE')    seg2 = 023.
if (seg = 'ADF')    seg2 = 024.
if (seg = 'AEA')    seg2 = 025.
if (seg = 'AEB')    seg2 = 026.
if (seg = 'AEC')    seg2 = 027.
if (seg = 'AED')    seg2 = 028.
if (seg = 'AEE')    seg2 = 029.
if (seg = 'AEF')    seg2 = 030.
if (seg = 'AFA')    seg2 = 031.
if (seg = 'AFB')    seg2 = 032.
if (seg = 'AFC')    seg2 = 033.
if (seg = 'AFD')    seg2 = 034.
if (seg = 'AFE')    seg2 = 035.
if (seg = 'AFF')    seg2 = 036.
if (seg = 'AGA')    seg2 = 037.
if (seg = 'AGB')    seg2 = 038.
if (seg = 'AGC')    seg2 = 039.
if (seg = 'AGD')    seg2 = 040.
if (seg = 'AGE')    seg2 = 041.
if (seg = 'AGF')    seg2 = 042.
if (seg = 'AHA')    seg2 = 043.
if (seg = 'AHB')    seg2 = 044.
if (seg = 'AHC')    seg2 = 045.
if (seg = 'AHD')    seg2 = 046.
if (seg = 'AHE')    seg2 = 047.
if (seg = 'AHF')    seg2 = 048.
if (seg = 'BAA')    seg2 = 049.
if (seg = 'BAB')    seg2 = 050.
if (seg = 'BAC')    seg2 = 051.
if (seg = 'BAD')    seg2 = 052.
if (seg = 'BAE')    seg2 = 053.
if (seg = 'BAF')    seg2 = 054.
if (seg = 'BBA')    seg2 = 055.
if (seg = 'BBB')    seg2 = 056.
if (seg = 'BBC')    seg2 = 057.
if (seg = 'BBD')    seg2 = 058.
if (seg = 'BBE')    seg2 = 059.
if (seg = 'BBF')    seg2 = 060.
if (seg = 'BCA')    seg2 = 061.
if (seg = 'BCB')    seg2 = 062.
if (seg = 'BCC')    seg2 = 063.
```

```
if (seg = 'BCD')   seg2 = 064.
if (seg = 'BCE')   seg2 = 065.
if (seg = 'BCF')   seg2 = 066.
if (seg = 'BDA')   seg2 = 067.
if (seg = 'BDB')   seg2 = 068.
if (seg = 'BDC')   seg2 = 069.
if (seg = 'BDD')   seg2 = 070.
if (seg = 'BDE')   seg2 = 071.
if (seg = 'BDF')   seg2 = 072.
if (seg = 'BEA')   seg2 = 073.
if (seg = 'BEB')   seg2 = 074.
if (seg = 'BEC')   seg2 = 075.
if (seg = 'BED')   seg2 = 076.
if (seg = 'BEE')   seg2 = 077.
if (seg = 'BEF')   seg2 = 078.
if (seg = 'BFA')   seg2 = 079.
if (seg = 'BFB')   seg2 = 080.
if (seg = 'BFC')   seg2 = 081.
if (seg = 'BFD')   seg2 = 082.
if (seg = 'BFE')   seg2 = 083.
if (seg = 'BFF')   seg2 = 084.
if (seg = 'BGA')   seg2 = 085.
if (seg = 'BGB')   seg2 = 086.
if (seg = 'BGC')   seg2 = 087.
if (seg = 'BGD')   seg2 = 088.
if (seg = 'BGE')   seg2 = 089.
if (seg = 'BGF')   seg2 = 090.
if (seg = 'BHA')   seg2 = 091.
if (seg = 'BHB')   seg2 = 092.
if (seg = 'BHC')   seg2 = 093.
if (seg = 'BHD')   seg2 = 094.
if (seg = 'BHE')   seg2 = 095.
if (seg = 'BHF')   seg2 = 096.
if (seg = 'CAA')   seg2 = 097.
if (seg = 'CAB')   seg2 = 098.
if (seg = 'CAC')   seg2 = 099.
if (seg = 'CAD')   seg2 = 100.
if (seg = 'CAE')   seg2 = 101.
if (seg = 'CAF')   seg2 = 102.
if (seg = 'CBA')   seg2 = 103.
if (seg = 'CBB')   seg2 = 104.
if (seg = 'CBC')   seg2 = 105.
if (seg = 'CBD')   seg2 = 106.
if (seg = 'CBE')   seg2 = 107.
if (seg = 'CBF')   seg2 = 108.
if (seg = 'CCA')   seg2 = 109.
if (seg = 'CCB')   seg2 = 110.
if (seg = 'CCC')   seg2 = 111.
if (seg = 'CCD')   seg2 = 112.
if (seg = 'CCE')   seg2 = 113.
if (seg = 'CCF')   seg2 = 114.
if (seg = 'CDA')   seg2 = 115.
if (seg = 'CDB')   seg2 = 116.
if (seg = 'CDC')   seg2 = 117.
if (seg = 'CDD')   seg2 = 118.
if (seg = 'CDE')   seg2 = 119.
if (seg = 'CDF')   seg2 = 120.
if (seg = 'CEA')   seg2 = 121.
if (seg = 'CEB')   seg2 = 122.
if (seg = 'CEC')   seg2 = 123.
if (seg = 'CED')   seg2 = 124.
if (seg = 'CEE')   seg2 = 125.
if (seg = 'CEF')   seg2 = 126.
if (seg = 'CFA')   seg2 = 127.
if (seg = 'CFB')   seg2 = 128.
if (seg = 'CFC')   seg2 = 129.
if (seg = 'CFD')   seg2 = 130.
```

```
if (seg = 'CFE')   seg2 = 131.
if (seg = 'CFF')   seg2 = 132.
if (seg = 'CGA')   seg2 = 133.
if (seg = 'CGB')   seg2 = 134.
if (seg = 'CGC')   seg2 = 135.
if (seg = 'CGD')   seg2 = 136.
if (seg = 'CGE')   seg2 = 137.
if (seg = 'CGF')   seg2 = 138.
if (seg = 'CHA')   seg2 = 139.
if (seg = 'CHB')   seg2 = 140.
if (seg = 'CHC')   seg2 = 141.
if (seg = 'CHD')   seg2 = 142.
if (seg = 'CHE')   seg2 = 143.
if (seg = 'CHF')   seg2 = 144.
if (seg = 'DAA')   seg2 = 145.
if (seg = 'DAB')   seg2 = 146.
if (seg = 'DAC')   seg2 = 147.
if (seg = 'DAD')   seg2 = 148.
if (seg = 'DAE')   seg2 = 149.
if (seg = 'DAF')   seg2 = 150.
if (seg = 'DBA')   seg2 = 151.
if (seg = 'DBB')   seg2 = 152.
if (seg = 'DBC')   seg2 = 153.
if (seg = 'DBD')   seg2 = 154.
if (seg = 'DBE')   seg2 = 155.
if (seg = 'DBF')   seg2 = 156.
if (seg = 'DCA')   seg2 = 157.
if (seg = 'DCB')   seg2 = 158.
if (seg = 'DCC')   seg2 = 159.
if (seg = 'DCD')   seg2 = 160.
if (seg = 'DCE')   seg2 = 161.
if (seg = 'DCF')   seg2 = 162.
if (seg = 'DDA')   seg2 = 163.
if (seg = 'DDB')   seg2 = 164.
if (seg = 'DDC')   seg2 = 165.
if (seg = 'DDD')   seg2 = 166.
if (seg = 'DDE')   seg2 = 167.
if (seg = 'DDF')   seg2 = 168.
if (seg = 'DEA')   seg2 = 169.
if (seg = 'DEB')   seg2 = 170.
if (seg = 'DEC')   seg2 = 171.
if (seg = 'DED')   seg2 = 172.
if (seg = 'DEE')   seg2 = 173.
if (seg = 'DEF')   seg2 = 174.
if (seg = 'DFA')   seg2 = 175.
if (seg = 'DFB')   seg2 = 176.
if (seg = 'DFC')   seg2 = 177.
if (seg = 'DFD')   seg2 = 178.
if (seg = 'DFE')   seg2 = 179.
if (seg = 'DFF')   seg2 = 180.
if (seg = 'DGA')   seg2 = 181.
if (seg = 'DGB')   seg2 = 182.
if (seg = 'DGC')   seg2 = 183.
if (seg = 'DGD')   seg2 = 184.
if (seg = 'DGE')   seg2 = 185.
if (seg = 'DGF')   seg2 = 186.
if (seg = 'DHA')   seg2 = 187.
if (seg = 'DHB')   seg2 = 188.
if (seg = 'DHC')   seg2 = 189.
if (seg = 'DHD')   seg2 = 190.
if (seg = 'DHE')   seg2 = 191.
if (seg = 'DHF')   seg2 = 192.
if (seg = 'FAA')   seg2 = 193.
if (seg = 'FAB')   seg2 = 194.
if (seg = 'FAC')   seg2 = 195.
if (seg = 'FAD')   seg2 = 196.
if (seg = 'FAE')   seg2 = 197.
```

```
if (seg = 'FAF')   seg2 = 198.
if (seg = 'FBA')   seg2 = 199.
if (seg = 'FBB')   seg2 = 200.
if (seg = 'FBC')   seg2 = 201.
if (seg = 'FBD')   seg2 = 202.
if (seg = 'FBE')   seg2 = 203.
if (seg = 'FBF')   seg2 = 204.
if (seg = 'FCA')   seg2 = 205.
if (seg = 'FCB')   seg2 = 206.
if (seg = 'FCC')   seg2 = 207.
if (seg = 'FCD')   seg2 = 208.
if (seg = 'FCE')   seg2 = 209.
if (seg = 'FCF')   seg2 = 210.
if (seg = 'FDA')   seg2 = 211.
if (seg = 'FDB')   seg2 = 212.
if (seg = 'FDC')   seg2 = 213.
if (seg = 'FDD')   seg2 = 214.
if (seg = 'FDE')   seg2 = 215.
if (seg = 'FDF')   seg2 = 216.
if (seg = 'FEA')   seg2 = 217.
if (seg = 'FEB')   seg2 = 218.
if (seg = 'FEC')   seg2 = 219.
if (seg = 'FED')   seg2 = 220.
if (seg = 'FEE')   seg2 = 221.
if (seg = 'FEF')   seg2 = 222.
if (seg = 'FFA')   seg2 = 223.
if (seg = 'FFB')   seg2 = 224.
if (seg = 'FFC')   seg2 = 225.
if (seg = 'FFD')   seg2 = 226.
if (seg = 'FFE')   seg2 = 227.
if (seg = 'FFF')   seg2 = 228.
if (seg = 'FGA')   seg2 = 229.
if (seg = 'FGB')   seg2 = 230.
if (seg = 'FGC')   seg2 = 231.
if (seg = 'FGD')   seg2 = 232.
if (seg = 'FGE')   seg2 = 233.
if (seg = 'FGF')   seg2 = 234.
if (seg = 'FHA')   seg2 = 235.
if (seg = 'FHB')   seg2 = 236.
if (seg = 'FHC')   seg2 = 237.
if (seg = 'FHD')   seg2 = 238.
if (seg = 'FHE')   seg2 = 239.
if (seg = 'FHF')   seg2 = 240.
*** Adjust For New Customers ***************.
if (gradep = 'ZZZZZZ')   seg1 = seg2 + 300.
formats seg1(f3.0) seg2(f3.0).
*** Now Create The Independent Variables ***.
compute fut000 = 0.
compute fut001 = 0.
compute fut002 = 0.
compute fut003 = 0.
compute fut004 = 0.
compute fut005 = 0.
compute fut006 = 0.
compute fut007 = 0.
compute fut008 = 0.
compute fut009 = 0.
compute fut010 = 0.
compute fut011 = 0.
compute fut012 = 0.
compute fut013 = 0.
compute fut014 = 0.
compute fut015 = 0.
compute fut016 = 0.
compute fut017 = 0.
compute fut018 = 0.
compute fut019 = 0.
```

132

```
compute fut020 = 0.
compute fut021 = 0.
compute fut022 = 0.
compute fut023 = 0.
compute fut024 = 0.
compute fut025 = 0.
compute fut026 = 0.
compute fut027 = 0.
compute fut028 = 0.
compute fut029 = 0.
compute fut030 = 0.
compute fut031 = 0.
compute fut032 = 0.
compute fut033 = 0.
compute fut034 = 0.
compute fut035 = 0.
compute fut036 = 0.
compute fut037 = 0.
compute fut038 = 0.
compute fut039 = 0.
compute fut040 = 0.
compute fut041 = 0.
compute fut042 = 0.
compute fut043 = 0.
compute fut044 = 0.
compute fut045 = 0.
compute fut046 = 0.
compute fut047 = 0.
compute fut048 = 0.
compute fut049 = 0.
compute fut050 = 0.
compute fut051 = 0.
compute fut052 = 0.
compute fut053 = 0.
compute fut054 = 0.
compute fut055 = 0.
compute fut056 = 0.
compute fut057 = 0.
compute fut058 = 0.
compute fut059 = 0.
compute fut060 = 0.
compute fut061 = 0.
compute fut062 = 0.
compute fut063 = 0.
compute fut064 = 0.
compute fut065 = 0.
compute fut066 = 0.
compute fut067 = 0.
compute fut068 = 0.
compute fut069 = 0.
compute fut070 = 0.
compute fut071 = 0.
compute fut072 = 0.
compute fut073 = 0.
compute fut074 = 0.
compute fut075 = 0.
compute fut076 = 0.
compute fut077 = 0.
compute fut078 = 0.
compute fut079 = 0.
compute fut080 = 0.
compute fut081 = 0.
compute fut082 = 0.
compute fut083 = 0.
compute fut084 = 0.
compute fut085 = 0.
compute fut086 = 0.
```

```
compute fut087 = 0.
compute fut088 = 0.
compute fut089 = 0.
compute fut090 = 0.
compute fut091 = 0.
compute fut092 = 0.
compute fut093 = 0.
compute fut094 = 0.
compute fut095 = 0.
compute fut096 = 0.
compute fut097 = 0.
compute fut098 = 0.
compute fut099 = 0.
compute fut100 = 0.
compute fut101 = 0.
compute fut102 = 0.
compute fut103 = 0.
compute fut104 = 0.
compute fut105 = 0.
compute fut106 = 0.
compute fut107 = 0.
compute fut108 = 0.
compute fut109 = 0.
compute fut110 = 0.
compute fut111 = 0.
compute fut112 = 0.
compute fut113 = 0.
compute fut114 = 0.
compute fut115 = 0.
compute fut116 = 0.
compute fut117 = 0.
compute fut118 = 0.
compute fut119 = 0.
compute fut120 = 0.
compute fut121 = 0.
compute fut122 = 0.
compute fut123 = 0.
compute fut124 = 0.
compute fut125 = 0.
compute fut126 = 0.
compute fut127 = 0.
compute fut128 = 0.
compute fut129 = 0.
compute fut130 = 0.
compute fut131 = 0.
compute fut132 = 0.
compute fut133 = 0.
compute fut134 = 0.
compute fut135 = 0.
compute fut136 = 0.
compute fut137 = 0.
compute fut138 = 0.
compute fut139 = 0.
compute fut140 = 0.
compute fut141 = 0.
compute fut142 = 0.
compute fut143 = 0.
compute fut144 = 0.
compute fut145 = 0.
compute fut146 = 0.
compute fut147 = 0.
compute fut148 = 0.
compute fut149 = 0.
compute fut150 = 0.
compute fut151 = 0.
compute fut152 = 0.
compute fut153 = 0.
```

```
compute fut154 = 0.
compute fut155 = 0.
compute fut156 = 0.
compute fut157 = 0.
compute fut158 = 0.
compute fut159 = 0.
compute fut160 = 0.
compute fut161 = 0.
compute fut162 = 0.
compute fut163 = 0.
compute fut164 = 0.
compute fut165 = 0.
compute fut166 = 0.
compute fut167 = 0.
compute fut168 = 0.
compute fut169 = 0.
compute fut170 = 0.
compute fut171 = 0.
compute fut172 = 0.
compute fut173 = 0.
compute fut174 = 0.
compute fut175 = 0.
compute fut176 = 0.
compute fut177 = 0.
compute fut178 = 0.
compute fut179 = 0.
compute fut180 = 0.
compute fut181 = 0.
compute fut182 = 0.
compute fut183 = 0.
compute fut184 = 0.
compute fut185 = 0.
compute fut186 = 0.
compute fut187 = 0.
compute fut188 = 0.
compute fut189 = 0.
compute fut190 = 0.
compute fut191 = 0.
compute fut192 = 0.
compute fut193 = 0.
compute fut194 = 0.
compute fut195 = 0.
compute fut196 = 0.
compute fut197 = 0.
compute fut198 = 0.
compute fut199 = 0.
compute fut200 = 0.
compute fut201 = 0.
compute fut202 = 0.
compute fut203 = 0.
compute fut204 = 0.
compute fut205 = 0.
compute fut206 = 0.
compute fut207 = 0.
compute fut208 = 0.
compute fut209 = 0.
compute fut210 = 0.
compute fut211 = 0.
compute fut212 = 0.
compute fut213 = 0.
compute fut214 = 0.
compute fut215 = 0.
compute fut216 = 0.
compute fut217 = 0.
compute fut218 = 0.
compute fut219 = 0.
compute fut220 = 0.
```

```
compute fut221 = 0.
compute fut222 = 0.
compute fut223 = 0.
compute fut224 = 0.
compute fut225 = 0.
compute fut226 = 0.
compute fut227 = 0.
compute fut228 = 0.
compute fut229 = 0.
compute fut230 = 0.
compute fut231 = 0.
compute fut232 = 0.
compute fut233 = 0.
compute fut234 = 0.
compute fut235 = 0.
compute fut236 = 0.
compute fut237 = 0.
compute fut238 = 0.
compute fut239 = 0.
compute fut240 = 0.
if (seg2 = 000)  fut000 = 1.
if (seg2 = 001)  fut001 = 1.
if (seg2 = 002)  fut002 = 1.
if (seg2 = 003)  fut003 = 1.
if (seg2 = 004)  fut004 = 1.
if (seg2 = 005)  fut005 = 1.
if (seg2 = 006)  fut006 = 1.
if (seg2 = 007)  fut007 = 1.
if (seg2 = 008)  fut008 = 1.
if (seg2 = 009)  fut009 = 1.
if (seg2 = 010)  fut010 = 1.
if (seg2 = 011)  fut011 = 1.
if (seg2 = 012)  fut012 = 1.
if (seg2 = 013)  fut013 = 1.
if (seg2 = 014)  fut014 = 1.
if (seg2 = 015)  fut015 = 1.
if (seg2 = 016)  fut016 = 1.
if (seg2 = 017)  fut017 = 1.
if (seg2 = 018)  fut018 = 1.
if (seg2 = 019)  fut019 = 1.
if (seg2 = 020)  fut020 = 1.
if (seg2 = 021)  fut021 = 1.
if (seg2 = 022)  fut022 = 1.
if (seg2 = 023)  fut023 = 1.
if (seg2 = 024)  fut024 = 1.
if (seg2 = 025)  fut025 = 1.
if (seg2 = 026)  fut026 = 1.
if (seg2 = 027)  fut027 = 1.
if (seg2 = 028)  fut028 = 1.
if (seg2 = 029)  fut029 = 1.
if (seg2 = 030)  fut030 = 1.
if (seg2 = 031)  fut031 = 1.
if (seg2 = 032)  fut032 = 1.
if (seg2 = 033)  fut033 = 1.
if (seg2 = 034)  fut034 = 1.
if (seg2 = 035)  fut035 = 1.
if (seg2 = 036)  fut036 = 1.
if (seg2 = 037)  fut037 = 1.
if (seg2 = 038)  fut038 = 1.
if (seg2 = 039)  fut039 = 1.
if (seg2 = 040)  fut040 = 1.
if (seg2 = 041)  fut041 = 1.
if (seg2 = 042)  fut042 = 1.
if (seg2 = 043)  fut043 = 1.
if (seg2 = 044)  fut044 = 1.
if (seg2 = 045)  fut045 = 1.
if (seg2 = 046)  fut046 = 1.
```

```
if (seg2 = 047)  fut047 = 1.
if (seg2 = 048)  fut048 = 1.
if (seg2 = 049)  fut049 = 1.
if (seg2 = 050)  fut050 = 1.
if (seg2 = 051)  fut051 = 1.
if (seg2 = 052)  fut052 = 1.
if (seg2 = 053)  fut053 = 1.
if (seg2 = 054)  fut054 = 1.
if (seg2 = 055)  fut055 = 1.
if (seg2 = 056)  fut056 = 1.
if (seg2 = 057)  fut057 = 1.
if (seg2 = 058)  fut058 = 1.
if (seg2 = 059)  fut059 = 1.
if (seg2 = 060)  fut060 = 1.
if (seg2 = 061)  fut061 = 1.
if (seg2 = 062)  fut062 = 1.
if (seg2 = 063)  fut063 = 1.
if (seg2 = 064)  fut064 = 1.
if (seg2 = 065)  fut065 = 1.
if (seg2 = 066)  fut066 = 1.
if (seg2 = 067)  fut067 = 1.
if (seg2 = 068)  fut068 = 1.
if (seg2 = 069)  fut069 = 1.
if (seg2 = 070)  fut070 = 1.
if (seg2 = 071)  fut071 = 1.
if (seg2 = 072)  fut072 = 1.
if (seg2 = 073)  fut073 = 1.
if (seg2 = 074)  fut074 = 1.
if (seg2 = 075)  fut075 = 1.
if (seg2 = 076)  fut076 = 1.
if (seg2 = 077)  fut077 = 1.
if (seg2 = 078)  fut078 = 1.
if (seg2 = 079)  fut079 = 1.
if (seg2 = 080)  fut080 = 1.
if (seg2 = 081)  fut081 = 1.
if (seg2 = 082)  fut082 = 1.
if (seg2 = 083)  fut083 = 1.
if (seg2 = 084)  fut084 = 1.
if (seg2 = 085)  fut085 = 1.
if (seg2 = 086)  fut086 = 1.
if (seg2 = 087)  fut087 = 1.
if (seg2 = 088)  fut088 = 1.
if (seg2 = 089)  fut089 = 1.
if (seg2 = 090)  fut090 = 1.
if (seg2 = 091)  fut091 = 1.
if (seg2 = 092)  fut092 = 1.
if (seg2 = 093)  fut093 = 1.
if (seg2 = 094)  fut094 = 1.
if (seg2 = 095)  fut095 = 1.
if (seg2 = 096)  fut096 = 1.
if (seg2 = 097)  fut097 = 1.
if (seg2 = 098)  fut098 = 1.
if (seg2 = 099)  fut099 = 1.
if (seg2 = 100)  fut100 = 1.
if (seg2 = 101)  fut101 = 1.
if (seg2 = 102)  fut102 = 1.
if (seg2 = 103)  fut103 = 1.
if (seg2 = 104)  fut104 = 1.
if (seg2 = 105)  fut105 = 1.
if (seg2 = 106)  fut106 = 1.
if (seg2 = 107)  fut107 = 1.
if (seg2 = 108)  fut108 = 1.
if (seg2 = 109)  fut109 = 1.
if (seg2 = 110)  fut110 = 1.
if (seg2 = 111)  fut111 = 1.
if (seg2 = 112)  fut112 = 1.
if (seg2 = 113)  fut113 = 1.
```

```
if (seg2 = 114)    fut114 = 1.
if (seg2 = 115)    fut115 = 1.
if (seg2 = 116)    fut116 = 1.
if (seg2 = 117)    fut117 = 1.
if (seg2 = 118)    fut118 = 1.
if (seg2 = 119)    fut119 = 1.
if (seg2 = 120)    fut120 = 1.
if (seg2 = 121)    fut121 = 1.
if (seg2 = 122)    fut122 = 1.
if (seg2 = 123)    fut123 = 1.
if (seg2 = 124)    fut124 = 1.
if (seg2 = 125)    fut125 = 1.
if (seg2 = 126)    fut126 = 1.
if (seg2 = 127)    fut127 = 1.
if (seg2 = 128)    fut128 = 1.
if (seg2 = 129)    fut129 = 1.
if (seg2 = 130)    fut130 = 1.
if (seg2 = 131)    fut131 = 1.
if (seg2 = 132)    fut132 = 1.
if (seg2 = 133)    fut133 = 1.
if (seg2 = 134)    fut134 = 1.
if (seg2 = 135)    fut135 = 1.
if (seg2 = 136)    fut136 = 1.
if (seg2 = 137)    fut137 = 1.
if (seg2 = 138)    fut138 = 1.
if (seg2 = 139)    fut139 = 1.
if (seg2 = 140)    fut140 = 1.
if (seg2 = 141)    fut141 = 1.
if (seg2 = 142)    fut142 = 1.
if (seg2 = 143)    fut143 = 1.
if (seg2 = 144)    fut144 = 1.
if (seg2 = 145)    fut145 = 1.
if (seg2 = 146)    fut146 = 1.
if (seg2 = 147)    fut147 = 1.
if (seg2 = 148)    fut148 = 1.
if (seg2 = 149)    fut149 = 1.
if (seg2 = 150)    fut150 = 1.
if (seg2 = 151)    fut151 = 1.
if (seg2 = 152)    fut152 = 1.
if (seg2 = 153)    fut153 = 1.
if (seg2 = 154)    fut154 = 1.
if (seg2 = 155)    fut155 = 1.
if (seg2 = 156)    fut156 = 1.
if (seg2 = 157)    fut157 = 1.
if (seg2 = 158)    fut158 = 1.
if (seg2 = 159)    fut159 = 1.
if (seg2 = 160)    fut160 = 1.
if (seg2 = 161)    fut161 = 1.
if (seg2 = 162)    fut162 = 1.
if (seg2 = 163)    fut163 = 1.
if (seg2 = 164)    fut164 = 1.
if (seg2 = 165)    fut165 = 1.
if (seg2 = 166)    fut166 = 1.
if (seg2 = 167)    fut167 = 1.
if (seg2 = 168)    fut168 = 1.
if (seg2 = 169)    fut169 = 1.
if (seg2 = 170)    fut170 = 1.
if (seg2 = 171)    fut171 = 1.
if (seg2 = 172)    fut172 = 1.
if (seg2 = 173)    fut173 = 1.
if (seg2 = 174)    fut174 = 1.
if (seg2 = 175)    fut175 = 1.
if (seg2 = 176)    fut176 = 1.
if (seg2 = 177)    fut177 = 1.
if (seg2 = 178)    fut178 = 1.
if (seg2 = 179)    fut179 = 1.
if (seg2 = 180)    fut180 = 1.
```

```
if (seg2 = 181)   fut181 = 1.
if (seg2 = 182)   fut182 = 1.
if (seg2 = 183)   fut183 = 1.
if (seg2 = 184)   fut184 = 1.
if (seg2 = 185)   fut185 = 1.
if (seg2 = 186)   fut186 = 1.
if (seg2 = 187)   fut187 = 1.
if (seg2 = 188)   fut188 = 1.
if (seg2 = 189)   fut189 = 1.
if (seg2 = 190)   fut190 = 1.
if (seg2 = 191)   fut191 = 1.
if (seg2 = 192)   fut192 = 1.
if (seg2 = 193)   fut193 = 1.
if (seg2 = 194)   fut194 = 1.
if (seg2 = 195)   fut195 = 1.
if (seg2 = 196)   fut196 = 1.
if (seg2 = 197)   fut197 = 1.
if (seg2 = 198)   fut198 = 1.
if (seg2 = 199)   fut199 = 1.
if (seg2 = 200)   fut200 = 1.
if (seg2 = 201)   fut201 = 1.
if (seg2 = 202)   fut202 = 1.
if (seg2 = 203)   fut203 = 1.
if (seg2 = 204)   fut204 = 1.
if (seg2 = 205)   fut205 = 1.
if (seg2 = 206)   fut206 = 1.
if (seg2 = 207)   fut207 = 1.
if (seg2 = 208)   fut208 = 1.
if (seg2 = 209)   fut209 = 1.
if (seg2 = 210)   fut210 = 1.
if (seg2 = 211)   fut211 = 1.
if (seg2 = 212)   fut212 = 1.
if (seg2 = 213)   fut213 = 1.
if (seg2 = 214)   fut214 = 1.
if (seg2 = 215)   fut215 = 1.
if (seg2 = 216)   fut216 = 1.
if (seg2 = 217)   fut217 = 1.
if (seg2 = 218)   fut218 = 1.
if (seg2 = 219)   fut219 = 1.
if (seg2 = 220)   fut220 = 1.
if (seg2 = 221)   fut221 = 1.
if (seg2 = 222)   fut222 = 1.
if (seg2 = 223)   fut223 = 1.
if (seg2 = 224)   fut224 = 1.
if (seg2 = 225)   fut225 = 1.
if (seg2 = 226)   fut226 = 1.
if (seg2 = 227)   fut227 = 1.
if (seg2 = 228)   fut228 = 1.
if (seg2 = 229)   fut229 = 1.
if (seg2 = 230)   fut230 = 1.
if (seg2 = 231)   fut231 = 1.
if (seg2 = 232)   fut232 = 1.
if (seg2 = 233)   fut233 = 1.
if (seg2 = 234)   fut234 = 1.
if (seg2 = 235)   fut235 = 1.
if (seg2 = 236)   fut236 = 1.
if (seg2 = 237)   fut237 = 1.
if (seg2 = 238)   fut238 = 1.
if (seg2 = 239)   fut239 = 1.
if (seg2 = 240)   fut240 = 1.
aggregate outfile = 'c:\datasets\dummy.sav'
  /break          = seg1 rebuy
  /cases          = n
  /fut000 fut001 fut002 fut003 fut004 fut005 fut006 fut007 fut008 fut009
   fut010 fut011 fut012 fut013 fut014 fut015 fut016 fut017 fut018 fut019
   fut020 fut021 fut022 fut023 fut024 fut025 fut026 fut027 fut028 fut029
   fut030 fut031 fut032 fut033 fut034 fut035 fut036 fut037 fut038 fut039
```

```
      fut040 fut041 fut042 fut043 fut044 fut045 fut046 fut047 fut048 fut049
      fut050 fut051 fut052 fut053 fut054 fut055 fut056 fut057 fut058 fut059
      fut060 fut061 fut062 fut063 fut064 fut065 fut066 fut067 fut068 fut069
      fut070 fut071 fut072 fut073 fut074 fut075 fut076 fut077 fut078 fut079
      fut080 fut081 fut082 fut083 fut084 fut085 fut086 fut087 fut088 fut089
      fut090 fut091 fut092 fut093 fut094 fut095 fut096 fut097 fut098 fut099
      fut100 fut101 fut102 fut103 fut104 fut105 fut106 fut107 fut108 fut109
      fut110 fut111 fut112 fut113 fut114 fut115 fut116 fut117 fut118 fut119
      fut120 fut121 fut122 fut123 fut124 fut125 fut126 fut127 fut128 fut129
      fut130 fut131 fut132 fut133 fut134 fut135 fut136 fut137 fut138 fut139
      fut140 fut141 fut142 fut143 fut144 fut145 fut146 fut147 fut148 fut149
      fut150 fut151 fut152 fut153 fut154 fut155 fut156 fut157 fut158 fut159
      fut160 fut161 fut162 fut163 fut164 fut165 fut166 fut167 fut168 fut169
      fut170 fut171 fut172 fut173 fut174 fut175 fut176 fut177 fut178 fut179
      fut180 fut181 fut182 fut183 fut184 fut185 fut186 fut187 fut188 fut189
      fut190 fut191 fut192 fut193 fut194 fut195 fut196 fut197 fut198 fut199
      fut200 fut201 fut202 fut203 fut204 fut205 fut206 fut207 fut208 fut209
      fut210 fut211 fut212 fut213 fut214 fut215 fut216 fut217 fut218 fut219
      fut220 fut221 fut222 fut223 fut224 fut225 fut226 fut227 fut228 fut229
      fut230 fut231 fut232 fut233 fut234 fut235 fut236 fut237 fut238 fut239
      fut240 = mean
(fut000 fut001 fut002 fut003 fut004 fut005 fut006 fut007 fut008 fut009
      fut010 fut011 fut012 fut013 fut014 fut015 fut016 fut017 fut018 fut019
      fut020 fut021 fut022 fut023 fut024 fut025 fut026 fut027 fut028 fut029
      fut030 fut031 fut032 fut033 fut034 fut035 fut036 fut037 fut038 fut039
      fut040 fut041 fut042 fut043 fut044 fut045 fut046 fut047 fut048 fut049
      fut050 fut051 fut052 fut053 fut054 fut055 fut056 fut057 fut058 fut059
      fut060 fut061 fut062 fut063 fut064 fut065 fut066 fut067 fut068 fut069
      fut070 fut071 fut072 fut073 fut074 fut075 fut076 fut077 fut078 fut079
      fut080 fut081 fut082 fut083 fut084 fut085 fut086 fut087 fut088 fut089
      fut090 fut091 fut092 fut093 fut094 fut095 fut096 fut097 fut098 fut099
      fut100 fut101 fut102 fut103 fut104 fut105 fut106 fut107 fut108 fut109
      fut110 fut111 fut112 fut113 fut114 fut115 fut116 fut117 fut118 fut119
      fut120 fut121 fut122 fut123 fut124 fut125 fut126 fut127 fut128 fut129
      fut130 fut131 fut132 fut133 fut134 fut135 fut136 fut137 fut138 fut139
      fut140 fut141 fut142 fut143 fut144 fut145 fut146 fut147 fut148 fut149
      fut150 fut151 fut152 fut153 fut154 fut155 fut156 fut157 fut158 fut159
      fut160 fut161 fut162 fut163 fut164 fut165 fut166 fut167 fut168 fut169
      fut170 fut171 fut172 fut173 fut174 fut175 fut176 fut177 fut178 fut179
      fut180 fut181 fut182 fut183 fut184 fut185 fut186 fut187 fut188 fut189
      fut190 fut191 fut192 fut193 fut194 fut195 fut196 fut197 fut198 fut199
      fut200 fut201 fut202 fut203 fut204 fut205 fut206 fut207 fut208 fut209
      fut210 fut211 fut212 fut213 fut214 fut215 fut216 fut217 fut218 fut219
      fut220 fut221 fut222 fut223 fut224 fut225 fut226 fut227 fut228 fut229
      fut230 fut231 fut232 fut233 fut234 fut235 fut236 fut237 fut238 fut239
      fut240)
      /buyr12 newb12 demd12 freq12 item12 = mean
      (buyr12 newb12 demd12 freq12 item12)
      /ind00 ind01 ind02 ind03 ind04 ind05 ind06 ind07 ind08 ind09
       ind10 ind11 ind12 ind13 ind14 ind15 ind16 ind17 ind18 ind19
       ind20 ind21 ind22 ind23 ind24 ind25 ind26 ind27 ind28 ind29
       ind30 ind31 ind32 ind33 ind34 ind35 ind36 ind37 ind38 ind39
       ind40 ind41 ind42 ind43 ind44 ind45 ind46 ind47 ind48 ind49
       ind50 ind51 ind52 ind53 ind54 ind55 ind56 ind57 ind58 ind59
       ind60 ind61 ind62 ind63 ind64 ind65 ind66 ind67 ind68 ind69
       ind70 ind71 ind72 ind73 ind74 ind75 ind76 ind77 ind78 ind79
       ind80 ind81 ind82 ind83 ind84 ind85 ind86 ind87 ind88 ind89
       ind90 ind91 ind92 ind93 ind94 ind95 ind96 ind97 ind98 ind99 = mean
      (ind00 ind01 ind02 ind03 ind04 ind05 ind06 ind07 ind08 ind09
       ind10 ind11 ind12 ind13 ind14 ind15 ind16 ind17 ind18 ind19
       ind20 ind21 ind22 ind23 ind24 ind25 ind26 ind27 ind28 ind29
       ind30 ind31 ind32 ind33 ind34 ind35 ind36 ind37 ind38 ind39
       ind40 ind41 ind42 ind43 ind44 ind45 ind46 ind47 ind48 ind49
       ind50 ind51 ind52 ind53 ind54 ind55 ind56 ind57 ind58 ind59
       ind60 ind61 ind62 ind63 ind64 ind65 ind66 ind67 ind68 ind69
       ind70 ind71 ind72 ind73 ind74 ind75 ind76 ind77 ind78 ind79
       ind80 ind81 ind82 ind83 ind84 ind85 ind86 ind87 ind88 ind89
```

```
                ind90 ind91 ind92 ind93 ind94 ind95 ind96 ind97 ind98 ind99).
select if (seg1 gt 0).
select if (seg1 le 240).
aggregate outfile = 'c:\datasets\dummy1.sav'
  /break          = rebuy
  /cases          = n
  /fut000 fut001 fut002 fut003 fut004 fut005 fut006 fut007 fut008 fut009
   fut010 fut011 fut012 fut013 fut014 fut015 fut016 fut017 fut018 fut019
   fut020 fut021 fut022 fut023 fut024 fut025 fut026 fut027 fut028 fut029
   fut030 fut031 fut032 fut033 fut034 fut035 fut036 fut037 fut038 fut039
   fut040 fut041 fut042 fut043 fut044 fut045 fut046 fut047 fut048 fut049
   fut050 fut051 fut052 fut053 fut054 fut055 fut056 fut057 fut058 fut059
   fut060 fut061 fut062 fut063 fut064 fut065 fut066 fut067 fut068 fut069
   fut070 fut071 fut072 fut073 fut074 fut075 fut076 fut077 fut078 fut079
   fut080 fut081 fut082 fut083 fut084 fut085 fut086 fut087 fut088 fut089
   fut090 fut091 fut092 fut093 fut094 fut095 fut096 fut097 fut098 fut099
   fut100 fut101 fut102 fut103 fut104 fut105 fut106 fut107 fut108 fut109
   fut110 fut111 fut112 fut113 fut114 fut115 fut116 fut117 fut118 fut119
   fut120 fut121 fut122 fut123 fut124 fut125 fut126 fut127 fut128 fut129
   fut130 fut131 fut132 fut133 fut134 fut135 fut136 fut137 fut138 fut139
   fut140 fut141 fut142 fut143 fut144 fut145 fut146 fut147 fut148 fut149
   fut150 fut151 fut152 fut153 fut154 fut155 fut156 fut157 fut158 fut159
   fut160 fut161 fut162 fut163 fut164 fut165 fut166 fut167 fut168 fut169
   fut170 fut171 fut172 fut173 fut174 fut175 fut176 fut177 fut178 fut179
   fut180 fut181 fut182 fut183 fut184 fut185 fut186 fut187 fut188 fut189
   fut190 fut191 fut192 fut193 fut194 fut195 fut196 fut197 fut198 fut199
   fut200 fut201 fut202 fut203 fut204 fut205 fut206 fut207 fut208 fut209
   fut210 fut211 fut212 fut213 fut214 fut215 fut216 fut217 fut218 fut219
   fut220 fut221 fut222 fut223 fut224 fut225 fut226 fut227 fut228 fut229
   fut230 fut231 fut232 fut233 fut234 fut235 fut236 fut237 fut238 fut239
   fut240 = mean
  (fut000 fut001 fut002 fut003 fut004 fut005 fut006 fut007 fut008 fut009
   fut010 fut011 fut012 fut013 fut014 fut015 fut016 fut017 fut018 fut019
   fut020 fut021 fut022 fut023 fut024 fut025 fut026 fut027 fut028 fut029
   fut030 fut031 fut032 fut033 fut034 fut035 fut036 fut037 fut038 fut039
   fut040 fut041 fut042 fut043 fut044 fut045 fut046 fut047 fut048 fut049
   fut050 fut051 fut052 fut053 fut054 fut055 fut056 fut057 fut058 fut059
   fut060 fut061 fut062 fut063 fut064 fut065 fut066 fut067 fut068 fut069
   fut070 fut071 fut072 fut073 fut074 fut075 fut076 fut077 fut078 fut079
   fut080 fut081 fut082 fut083 fut084 fut085 fut086 fut087 fut088 fut089
   fut090 fut091 fut092 fut093 fut094 fut095 fut096 fut097 fut098 fut099
   fut100 fut101 fut102 fut103 fut104 fut105 fut106 fut107 fut108 fut109
   fut110 fut111 fut112 fut113 fut114 fut115 fut116 fut117 fut118 fut119
   fut120 fut121 fut122 fut123 fut124 fut125 fut126 fut127 fut128 fut129
   fut130 fut131 fut132 fut133 fut134 fut135 fut136 fut137 fut138 fut139
   fut140 fut141 fut142 fut143 fut144 fut145 fut146 fut147 fut148 fut149
   fut150 fut151 fut152 fut153 fut154 fut155 fut156 fut157 fut158 fut159
   fut160 fut161 fut162 fut163 fut164 fut165 fut166 fut167 fut168 fut169
   fut170 fut171 fut172 fut173 fut174 fut175 fut176 fut177 fut178 fut179
   fut180 fut181 fut182 fut183 fut184 fut185 fut186 fut187 fut188 fut189
   fut190 fut191 fut192 fut193 fut194 fut195 fut196 fut197 fut198 fut199
   fut200 fut201 fut202 fut203 fut204 fut205 fut206 fut207 fut208 fut209
   fut210 fut211 fut212 fut213 fut214 fut215 fut216 fut217 fut218 fut219
   fut220 fut221 fut222 fut223 fut224 fut225 fut226 fut227 fut228 fut229
   fut230 fut231 fut232 fut233 fut234 fut235 fut236 fut237 fut238 fut239
   fut240)
        /buyr12 newb12 demd12 freq12 item12 = mean
        (buyr12 newb12 demd12 freq12 item12)
        /ind00 ind01 ind02 ind03 ind04 ind05 ind06 ind07 ind08 ind09
         ind10 ind11 ind12 ind13 ind14 ind15 ind16 ind17 ind18 ind19
         ind20 ind21 ind22 ind23 ind24 ind25 ind26 ind27 ind28 ind29
         ind30 ind31 ind32 ind33 ind34 ind35 ind36 ind37 ind38 ind39
         ind40 ind41 ind42 ind43 ind44 ind45 ind46 ind47 ind48 ind49
         ind50 ind51 ind52 ind53 ind54 ind55 ind56 ind57 ind58 ind59
         ind60 ind61 ind62 ind63 ind64 ind65 ind66 ind67 ind68 ind69
         ind70 ind71 ind72 ind73 ind74 ind75 ind76 ind77 ind78 ind79
         ind80 ind81 ind82 ind83 ind84 ind85 ind86 ind87 ind88 ind89
```

```
               ind90 ind91 ind92 ind93 ind94 ind95 ind96 ind97 ind98 ind99 = mean
              (ind00 ind01 ind02 ind03 ind04 ind05 ind06 ind07 ind08 ind09
               ind10 ind11 ind12 ind13 ind14 ind15 ind16 ind17 ind18 ind19
               ind20 ind21 ind22 ind23 ind24 ind25 ind26 ind27 ind28 ind29
               ind30 ind31 ind32 ind33 ind34 ind35 ind36 ind37 ind38 ind39
               ind40 ind41 ind42 ind43 ind44 ind45 ind46 ind47 ind48 ind49
               ind50 ind51 ind52 ind53 ind54 ind55 ind56 ind57 ind58 ind59
               ind60 ind61 ind62 ind63 ind64 ind65 ind66 ind67 ind68 ind69
               ind70 ind71 ind72 ind73 ind74 ind75 ind76 ind77 ind78 ind79
               ind80 ind81 ind82 ind83 ind84 ind85 ind86 ind87 ind88 ind89
               ind90 ind91 ind92 ind93 ind94 ind95 ind96 ind97 ind98 ind99).
execute.
*** Create Missing Segments Dataset
**********************************************.
compute #a = #a + 1.
compute order = #a.
execute.
select if (order le 240).
compute rebuy = 0.
save outfile = 'c:\datasets\dummy2.sav'
        /keep = order rebuy.
compute rebuy = 1.
save outfile = 'c:\datasets\dummy3.sav'
        /keep = order rebuy.
execute.
compute order = order + 300.
save outfile = 'c:\datasets\dummy4.sav'
        /keep = order rebuy.
execute.
add files  file = 'c:\datasets\dummy2.sav'
          /file = 'c:\datasets\dummy3.sav'
          /file = 'c:\datasets\dummy4.sav'
            /by = order rebuy.
compute seg1 = order.
formats seg1(f3.0).
save outfile = 'c:\datasets\dummy4.sav'
        /keep = seg1 rebuy.
execute.
*** Now Match Files Together
*****************************************************.
match files  file = 'c:\datasets\dummy.sav'
            /file = 'c:\datasets\dummy4.sav'
              /by = seg1 rebuy.
if missing(cases)  cases = 0.
aggregate outfile = 'c:\datasets\dummy5.sav'
        /break            = seg1
        /totcases         = sum(cases).
match files  file = *
            /table = 'c:\datasets\dummy5.sav'
              /by = seg1.
execute.
save outfile = 'c:\datasets\dummy5.sav'.
execute.
*** Select Segments With File Counts
*********************************************.
get file = 'c:\datasets\dummy5.sav'.
select if (totcases ne 0).
do if cases = 0.
compute fut000 = 0.
compute fut001 = 0.
compute fut002 = 0.
compute fut003 = 0.
compute fut004 = 0.
compute fut005 = 0.
compute fut006 = 0.
compute fut007 = 0.
compute fut008 = 0.
```

```
compute fut009 = 0.
compute fut010 = 0.
compute fut011 = 0.
compute fut012 = 0.
compute fut013 = 0.
compute fut014 = 0.
compute fut015 = 0.
compute fut016 = 0.
compute fut017 = 0.
compute fut018 = 0.
compute fut019 = 0.
compute fut020 = 0.
compute fut021 = 0.
compute fut022 = 0.
compute fut023 = 0.
compute fut024 = 0.
compute fut025 = 0.
compute fut026 = 0.
compute fut027 = 0.
compute fut028 = 0.
compute fut029 = 0.
compute fut030 = 0.
compute fut031 = 0.
compute fut032 = 0.
compute fut033 = 0.
compute fut034 = 0.
compute fut035 = 0.
compute fut036 = 0.
compute fut037 = 0.
compute fut038 = 0.
compute fut039 = 0.
compute fut040 = 0.
compute fut041 = 0.
compute fut042 = 0.
compute fut043 = 0.
compute fut044 = 0.
compute fut045 = 0.
compute fut046 = 0.
compute fut047 = 0.
compute fut048 = 0.
compute fut049 = 0.
compute fut050 = 0.
compute fut051 = 0.
compute fut052 = 0.
compute fut053 = 0.
compute fut054 = 0.
compute fut055 = 0.
compute fut056 = 0.
compute fut057 = 0.
compute fut058 = 0.
compute fut059 = 0.
compute fut060 = 0.
compute fut061 = 0.
compute fut062 = 0.
compute fut063 = 0.
compute fut064 = 0.
compute fut065 = 0.
compute fut066 = 0.
compute fut067 = 0.
compute fut068 = 0.
compute fut069 = 0.
compute fut070 = 0.
compute fut071 = 0.
compute fut072 = 0.
compute fut073 = 0.
compute fut074 = 0.
compute fut075 = 0.
```

```
compute fut076 = 0.
compute fut077 = 0.
compute fut078 = 0.
compute fut079 = 0.
compute fut080 = 0.
compute fut081 = 0.
compute fut082 = 0.
compute fut083 = 0.
compute fut084 = 0.
compute fut085 = 0.
compute fut086 = 0.
compute fut087 = 0.
compute fut088 = 0.
compute fut089 = 0.
compute fut090 = 0.
compute fut091 = 0.
compute fut092 = 0.
compute fut093 = 0.
compute fut094 = 0.
compute fut095 = 0.
compute fut096 = 0.
compute fut097 = 0.
compute fut098 = 0.
compute fut099 = 0.
compute fut100 = 0.
compute fut101 = 0.
compute fut102 = 0.
compute fut103 = 0.
compute fut104 = 0.
compute fut105 = 0.
compute fut106 = 0.
compute fut107 = 0.
compute fut108 = 0.
compute fut109 = 0.
compute fut110 = 0.
compute fut111 = 0.
compute fut112 = 0.
compute fut113 = 0.
compute fut114 = 0.
compute fut115 = 0.
compute fut116 = 0.
compute fut117 = 0.
compute fut118 = 0.
compute fut119 = 0.
compute fut120 = 0.
compute fut121 = 0.
compute fut122 = 0.
compute fut123 = 0.
compute fut124 = 0.
compute fut125 = 0.
compute fut126 = 0.
compute fut127 = 0.
compute fut128 = 0.
compute fut129 = 0.
compute fut130 = 0.
compute fut131 = 0.
compute fut132 = 0.
compute fut133 = 0.
compute fut134 = 0.
compute fut135 = 0.
compute fut136 = 0.
compute fut137 = 0.
compute fut138 = 0.
compute fut139 = 0.
compute fut140 = 0.
compute fut141 = 0.
compute fut142 = 0.
```

```
compute fut143 = 0.
compute fut144 = 0.
compute fut145 = 0.
compute fut146 = 0.
compute fut147 = 0.
compute fut148 = 0.
compute fut149 = 0.
compute fut150 = 0.
compute fut151 = 0.
compute fut152 = 0.
compute fut153 = 0.
compute fut154 = 0.
compute fut155 = 0.
compute fut156 = 0.
compute fut157 = 0.
compute fut158 = 0.
compute fut159 = 0.
compute fut160 = 0.
compute fut161 = 0.
compute fut162 = 0.
compute fut163 = 0.
compute fut164 = 0.
compute fut165 = 0.
compute fut166 = 0.
compute fut167 = 0.
compute fut168 = 0.
compute fut169 = 0.
compute fut170 = 0.
compute fut171 = 0.
compute fut172 = 0.
compute fut173 = 0.
compute fut174 = 0.
compute fut175 = 0.
compute fut176 = 0.
compute fut177 = 0.
compute fut178 = 0.
compute fut179 = 0.
compute fut180 = 0.
compute fut181 = 0.
compute fut182 = 0.
compute fut183 = 0.
compute fut184 = 0.
compute fut185 = 0.
compute fut186 = 0.
compute fut187 = 0.
compute fut188 = 0.
compute fut189 = 0.
compute fut190 = 0.
compute fut191 = 0.
compute fut192 = 0.
compute fut193 = 0.
compute fut194 = 0.
compute fut195 = 0.
compute fut196 = 0.
compute fut197 = 0.
compute fut198 = 0.
compute fut199 = 0.
compute fut200 = 0.
compute fut201 = 0.
compute fut202 = 0.
compute fut203 = 0.
compute fut204 = 0.
compute fut205 = 0.
compute fut206 = 0.
compute fut207 = 0.
compute fut208 = 0.
compute fut209 = 0.
```

```
compute fut210 = 0.
compute fut211 = 0.
compute fut212 = 0.
compute fut213 = 0.
compute fut214 = 0.
compute fut215 = 0.
compute fut216 = 0.
compute fut217 = 0.
compute fut218 = 0.
compute fut219 = 0.
compute fut220 = 0.
compute fut221 = 0.
compute fut222 = 0.
compute fut223 = 0.
compute fut224 = 0.
compute fut225 = 0.
compute fut226 = 0.
compute fut227 = 0.
compute fut228 = 0.
compute fut229 = 0.
compute fut230 = 0.
compute fut231 = 0.
compute fut232 = 0.
compute fut233 = 0.
compute fut234 = 0.
compute fut235 = 0.
compute fut236 = 0.
compute fut237 = 0.
compute fut238 = 0.
compute fut239 = 0.
compute fut240 = 0.
compute buyr12 = 0.
compute newb12 = 0.
compute demd12 = 0.
compute freq12 = 0.
compute item12 = 0.
compute ind00  = 0.
compute ind01  = 0.
compute ind02  = 0.
compute ind03  = 0.
compute ind04  = 0.
compute ind05  = 0.
compute ind06  = 0.
compute ind07  = 0.
compute ind08  = 0.
compute ind09  = 0.
compute ind10  = 0.
compute ind11  = 0.
compute ind12  = 0.
compute ind13  = 0.
compute ind14  = 0.
compute ind15  = 0.
compute ind16  = 0.
compute ind17  = 0.
compute ind18  = 0.
compute ind19  = 0.
compute ind20  = 0.
compute ind21  = 0.
compute ind22  = 0.
compute ind23  = 0.
compute ind24  = 0.
compute ind25  = 0.
compute ind26  = 0.
compute ind27  = 0.
compute ind28  = 0.
compute ind29  = 0.
compute ind30  = 0.
```

```
compute ind31  = 0.
compute ind32  = 0.
compute ind33  = 0.
compute ind34  = 0.
compute ind35  = 0.
compute ind36  = 0.
compute ind37  = 0.
compute ind38  = 0.
compute ind39  = 0.
compute ind40  = 0.
compute ind41  = 0.
compute ind42  = 0.
compute ind43  = 0.
compute ind44  = 0.
compute ind45  = 0.
compute ind46  = 0.
compute ind47  = 0.
compute ind48  = 0.
compute ind49  = 0.
compute ind50  = 0.
compute ind51  = 0.
compute ind52  = 0.
compute ind53  = 0.
compute ind54  = 0.
compute ind55  = 0.
compute ind56  = 0.
compute ind57  = 0.
compute ind58  = 0.
compute ind59  = 0.
compute ind60  = 0.
compute ind61  = 0.
compute ind62  = 0.
compute ind63  = 0.
compute ind64  = 0.
compute ind65  = 0.
compute ind66  = 0.
compute ind67  = 0.
compute ind68  = 0.
compute ind69  = 0.
compute ind70  = 0.
compute ind71  = 0.
compute ind72  = 0.
compute ind73  = 0.
compute ind74  = 0.
compute ind75  = 0.
compute ind76  = 0.
compute ind77  = 0.
compute ind78  = 0.
compute ind79  = 0.
compute ind80  = 0.
compute ind81  = 0.
compute ind82  = 0.
compute ind83  = 0.
compute ind84  = 0.
compute ind85  = 0.
compute ind86  = 0.
compute ind87  = 0.
compute ind88  = 0.
compute ind89  = 0.
compute ind90  = 0.
compute ind91  = 0.
compute ind92  = 0.
compute ind93  = 0.
compute ind94  = 0.
compute ind95  = 0.
compute ind96  = 0.
compute ind97  = 0.
```

```
compute ind98  = 0.
compute ind99  = 0.
end if.
save outfile = 'c:\datasets\dummy6.sav'.
execute.
*** Select Segments With No File Counts
*******************************************.
get file = 'c:\datasets\dummy5.sav'
          /keep = seg1 rebuy totcases.
select if (totcases eq 0).
sort cases by rebuy.
match files  file = *
             /table = 'c:\datasets\dummy1.sav'
             /by = rebuy.
sort cases by seg1.
do if seg1 ge 300.
compute cases  = 0.
compute fut000 = 0.
compute fut001 = 0.
compute fut002 = 0.
compute fut003 = 0.
compute fut004 = 0.
compute fut005 = 0.
compute fut006 = 0.
compute fut007 = 0.
compute fut008 = 0.
compute fut009 = 0.
compute fut010 = 0.
compute fut011 = 0.
compute fut012 = 0.
compute fut013 = 0.
compute fut014 = 0.
compute fut015 = 0.
compute fut016 = 0.
compute fut017 = 0.
compute fut018 = 0.
compute fut019 = 0.
compute fut020 = 0.
compute fut021 = 0.
compute fut022 = 0.
compute fut023 = 0.
compute fut024 = 0.
compute fut025 = 0.
compute fut026 = 0.
compute fut027 = 0.
compute fut028 = 0.
compute fut029 = 0.
compute fut030 = 0.
compute fut031 = 0.
compute fut032 = 0.
compute fut033 = 0.
compute fut034 = 0.
compute fut035 = 0.
compute fut036 = 0.
compute fut037 = 0.
compute fut038 = 0.
compute fut039 = 0.
compute fut040 = 0.
compute fut041 = 0.
compute fut042 = 0.
compute fut043 = 0.
compute fut044 = 0.
compute fut045 = 0.
compute fut046 = 0.
compute fut047 = 0.
compute fut048 = 0.
compute fut049 = 0.
```

```
compute fut050 = 0.
compute fut051 = 0.
compute fut052 = 0.
compute fut053 = 0.
compute fut054 = 0.
compute fut055 = 0.
compute fut056 = 0.
compute fut057 = 0.
compute fut058 = 0.
compute fut059 = 0.
compute fut060 = 0.
compute fut061 = 0.
compute fut062 = 0.
compute fut063 = 0.
compute fut064 = 0.
compute fut065 = 0.
compute fut066 = 0.
compute fut067 = 0.
compute fut068 = 0.
compute fut069 = 0.
compute fut070 = 0.
compute fut071 = 0.
compute fut072 = 0.
compute fut073 = 0.
compute fut074 = 0.
compute fut075 = 0.
compute fut076 = 0.
compute fut077 = 0.
compute fut078 = 0.
compute fut079 = 0.
compute fut080 = 0.
compute fut081 = 0.
compute fut082 = 0.
compute fut083 = 0.
compute fut084 = 0.
compute fut085 = 0.
compute fut086 = 0.
compute fut087 = 0.
compute fut088 = 0.
compute fut089 = 0.
compute fut090 = 0.
compute fut091 = 0.
compute fut092 = 0.
compute fut093 = 0.
compute fut094 = 0.
compute fut095 = 0.
compute fut096 = 0.
compute fut097 = 0.
compute fut098 = 0.
compute fut099 = 0.
compute fut100 = 0.
compute fut101 = 0.
compute fut102 = 0.
compute fut103 = 0.
compute fut104 = 0.
compute fut105 = 0.
compute fut106 = 0.
compute fut107 = 0.
compute fut108 = 0.
compute fut109 = 0.
compute fut110 = 0.
compute fut111 = 0.
compute fut112 = 0.
compute fut113 = 0.
compute fut114 = 0.
compute fut115 = 0.
compute fut116 = 0.
```

```
compute fut117 = 0.
compute fut118 = 0.
compute fut119 = 0.
compute fut120 = 0.
compute fut121 = 0.
compute fut122 = 0.
compute fut123 = 0.
compute fut124 = 0.
compute fut125 = 0.
compute fut126 = 0.
compute fut127 = 0.
compute fut128 = 0.
compute fut129 = 0.
compute fut130 = 0.
compute fut131 = 0.
compute fut132 = 0.
compute fut133 = 0.
compute fut134 = 0.
compute fut135 = 0.
compute fut136 = 0.
compute fut137 = 0.
compute fut138 = 0.
compute fut139 = 0.
compute fut140 = 0.
compute fut141 = 0.
compute fut142 = 0.
compute fut143 = 0.
compute fut144 = 0.
compute fut145 = 0.
compute fut146 = 0.
compute fut147 = 0.
compute fut148 = 0.
compute fut149 = 0.
compute fut150 = 0.
compute fut151 = 0.
compute fut152 = 0.
compute fut153 = 0.
compute fut154 = 0.
compute fut155 = 0.
compute fut156 = 0.
compute fut157 = 0.
compute fut158 = 0.
compute fut159 = 0.
compute fut160 = 0.
compute fut161 = 0.
compute fut162 = 0.
compute fut163 = 0.
compute fut164 = 0.
compute fut165 = 0.
compute fut166 = 0.
compute fut167 = 0.
compute fut168 = 0.
compute fut169 = 0.
compute fut170 = 0.
compute fut171 = 0.
compute fut172 = 0.
compute fut173 = 0.
compute fut174 = 0.
compute fut175 = 0.
compute fut176 = 0.
compute fut177 = 0.
compute fut178 = 0.
compute fut179 = 0.
compute fut180 = 0.
compute fut181 = 0.
compute fut182 = 0.
compute fut183 = 0.
```

```
compute fut184 = 0.
compute fut185 = 0.
compute fut186 = 0.
compute fut187 = 0.
compute fut188 = 0.
compute fut189 = 0.
compute fut190 = 0.
compute fut191 = 0.
compute fut192 = 0.
compute fut193 = 0.
compute fut194 = 0.
compute fut195 = 0.
compute fut196 = 0.
compute fut197 = 0.
compute fut198 = 0.
compute fut199 = 0.
compute fut200 = 0.
compute fut201 = 0.
compute fut202 = 0.
compute fut203 = 0.
compute fut204 = 0.
compute fut205 = 0.
compute fut206 = 0.
compute fut207 = 0.
compute fut208 = 0.
compute fut209 = 0.
compute fut210 = 0.
compute fut211 = 0.
compute fut212 = 0.
compute fut213 = 0.
compute fut214 = 0.
compute fut215 = 0.
compute fut216 = 0.
compute fut217 = 0.
compute fut218 = 0.
compute fut219 = 0.
compute fut220 = 0.
compute fut221 = 0.
compute fut222 = 0.
compute fut223 = 0.
compute fut224 = 0.
compute fut225 = 0.
compute fut226 = 0.
compute fut227 = 0.
compute fut228 = 0.
compute fut229 = 0.
compute fut230 = 0.
compute fut231 = 0.
compute fut232 = 0.
compute fut233 = 0.
compute fut234 = 0.
compute fut235 = 0.
compute fut236 = 0.
compute fut237 = 0.
compute fut238 = 0.
compute fut239 = 0.
compute fut240 = 0.
compute buyr12 = 0.
compute newb12 = 0.
compute demd12 = 0.
compute freq12 = 0.
compute item12 = 0.
compute ind00  = 0.
compute ind01  = 0.
compute ind02  = 0.
compute ind03  = 0.
compute ind04  = 0.
```

```
compute ind05   = 0.
compute ind06   = 0.
compute ind07   = 0.
compute ind08   = 0.
compute ind09   = 0.
compute ind10   = 0.
compute ind11   = 0.
compute ind12   = 0.
compute ind13   = 0.
compute ind14   = 0.
compute ind15   = 0.
compute ind16   = 0.
compute ind17   = 0.
compute ind18   = 0.
compute ind19   = 0.
compute ind20   = 0.
compute ind21   = 0.
compute ind22   = 0.
compute ind23   = 0.
compute ind24   = 0.
compute ind25   = 0.
compute ind26   = 0.
compute ind27   = 0.
compute ind28   = 0.
compute ind29   = 0.
compute ind30   = 0.
compute ind31   = 0.
compute ind32   = 0.
compute ind33   = 0.
compute ind34   = 0.
compute ind35   = 0.
compute ind36   = 0.
compute ind37   = 0.
compute ind38   = 0.
compute ind39   = 0.
compute ind40   = 0.
compute ind41   = 0.
compute ind42   = 0.
compute ind43   = 0.
compute ind44   = 0.
compute ind45   = 0.
compute ind46   = 0.
compute ind47   = 0.
compute ind48   = 0.
compute ind49   = 0.
compute ind50   = 0.
compute ind51   = 0.
compute ind52   = 0.
compute ind53   = 0.
compute ind54   = 0.
compute ind55   = 0.
compute ind56   = 0.
compute ind57   = 0.
compute ind58   = 0.
compute ind59   = 0.
compute ind60   = 0.
compute ind61   = 0.
compute ind62   = 0.
compute ind63   = 0.
compute ind64   = 0.
compute ind65   = 0.
compute ind66   = 0.
compute ind67   = 0.
compute ind68   = 0.
compute ind69   = 0.
compute ind70   = 0.
compute ind71   = 0.
```

```
compute ind72  = 0.
compute ind73  = 0.
compute ind74  = 0.
compute ind75  = 0.
compute ind76  = 0.
compute ind77  = 0.
compute ind78  = 0.
compute ind79  = 0.
compute ind80  = 0.
compute ind81  = 0.
compute ind82  = 0.
compute ind83  = 0.
compute ind84  = 0.
compute ind85  = 0.
compute ind86  = 0.
compute ind87  = 0.
compute ind88  = 0.
compute ind89  = 0.
compute ind90  = 0.
compute ind91  = 0.
compute ind92  = 0.
compute ind93  = 0.
compute ind94  = 0.
compute ind95  = 0.
compute ind96  = 0.
compute ind97  = 0.
compute ind98  = 0.
compute ind99  = 0.
end if.
save outfile = 'c:\datasets\dummy7.sav'.
execute.
*** Now Re-Integrate The Two Datasets
*********************************************.
add files  file = 'c:\datasets\dummy6.sav'
          /file = 'c:\datasets\dummy7.sav'.
sort cases by seg1.
sort cases by rebuy(d).
SAVE TRANSLATE OUTFILE='C:\datasets\oms.csv'
   /TYPE=csv /MAP /REPLACE /FIELDNAMES
   /CELLS=VALUES.
execute.

**********************************************************************************
*.
*** Copy Contents Of OMS.CSV, Plug It Into The OMS Spreadsheet At A1500
*****.
**********************************************************************************
*.


*** Beginning File Counts ***.
get file = 'c:\datasets\OMS6.sav'
        /keep = household_id gradep gradef.
*** Historical Segments First ***.
string seg(a6).
compute seg = gradep.
compute seg1 = 0.
if (seg = 'AAA')  seg1 = 001.
if (seg = 'AAB')  seg1 = 002.
if (seg = 'AAC')  seg1 = 003.
if (seg = 'AAD')  seg1 = 004.
if (seg = 'AAE')  seg1 = 005.
if (seg = 'AAF')  seg1 = 006.
if (seg = 'ABA')  seg1 = 007.
if (seg = 'ABB')  seg1 = 008.
if (seg = 'ABC')  seg1 = 009.
if (seg = 'ABD')  seg1 = 010.
```

153

```
if (seg = 'ABE')   seg1 = 011.
if (seg = 'ABF')   seg1 = 012.
if (seg = 'ACA')   seg1 = 013.
if (seg = 'ACB')   seg1 = 014.
if (seg = 'ACC')   seg1 = 015.
if (seg = 'ACD')   seg1 = 016.
if (seg = 'ACE')   seg1 = 017.
if (seg = 'ACF')   seg1 = 018.
if (seg = 'ADA')   seg1 = 019.
if (seg = 'ADB')   seg1 = 020.
if (seg = 'ADC')   seg1 = 021.
if (seg = 'ADD')   seg1 = 022.
if (seg = 'ADE')   seg1 = 023.
if (seg = 'ADF')   seg1 = 024.
if (seg = 'AEA')   seg1 = 025.
if (seg = 'AEB')   seg1 = 026.
if (seg = 'AEC')   seg1 = 027.
if (seg = 'AED')   seg1 = 028.
if (seg = 'AEE')   seg1 = 029.
if (seg = 'AEF')   seg1 = 030.
if (seg = 'AFA')   seg1 = 031.
if (seg = 'AFB')   seg1 = 032.
if (seg = 'AFC')   seg1 = 033.
if (seg = 'AFD')   seg1 = 034.
if (seg = 'AFE')   seg1 = 035.
if (seg = 'AFF')   seg1 = 036.
if (seg = 'AGA')   seg1 = 037.
if (seg = 'AGB')   seg1 = 038.
if (seg = 'AGC')   seg1 = 039.
if (seg = 'AGD')   seg1 = 040.
if (seg = 'AGE')   seg1 = 041.
if (seg = 'AGF')   seg1 = 042.
if (seg = 'AHA')   seg1 = 043.
if (seg = 'AHB')   seg1 = 044.
if (seg = 'AHC')   seg1 = 045.
if (seg = 'AHD')   seg1 = 046.
if (seg = 'AHE')   seg1 = 047.
if (seg = 'AHF')   seg1 = 048.
if (seg = 'BAA')   seg1 = 049.
if (seg = 'BAB')   seg1 = 050.
if (seg = 'BAC')   seg1 = 051.
if (seg = 'BAD')   seg1 = 052.
if (seg = 'BAE')   seg1 = 053.
if (seg = 'BAF')   seg1 = 054.
if (seg = 'BBA')   seg1 = 055.
if (seg = 'BBB')   seg1 = 056.
if (seg = 'BBC')   seg1 = 057.
if (seg = 'BBD')   seg1 = 058.
if (seg = 'BBE')   seg1 = 059.
if (seg = 'BBF')   seg1 = 060.
if (seg = 'BCA')   seg1 = 061.
if (seg = 'BCB')   seg1 = 062.
if (seg = 'BCC')   seg1 = 063.
if (seg = 'BCD')   seg1 = 064.
if (seg = 'BCE')   seg1 = 065.
if (seg = 'BCF')   seg1 = 066.
if (seg = 'BDA')   seg1 = 067.
if (seg = 'BDB')   seg1 = 068.
if (seg = 'BDC')   seg1 = 069.
if (seg = 'BDD')   seg1 = 070.
if (seg = 'BDE')   seg1 = 071.
if (seg = 'BDF')   seg1 = 072.
if (seg = 'BEA')   seg1 = 073.
if (seg = 'BEB')   seg1 = 074.
if (seg = 'BEC')   seg1 = 075.
if (seg = 'BED')   seg1 = 076.
if (seg = 'BEE')   seg1 = 077.
```

```
if (seg = 'BEF')   seg1 = 078.
if (seg = 'BFA')   seg1 = 079.
if (seg = 'BFB')   seg1 = 080.
if (seg = 'BFC')   seg1 = 081.
if (seg = 'BFD')   seg1 = 082.
if (seg = 'BFE')   seg1 = 083.
if (seg = 'BFF')   seg1 = 084.
if (seg = 'BGA')   seg1 = 085.
if (seg = 'BGB')   seg1 = 086.
if (seg = 'BGC')   seg1 = 087.
if (seg = 'BGD')   seg1 = 088.
if (seg = 'BGE')   seg1 = 089.
if (seg = 'BGF')   seg1 = 090.
if (seg = 'BHA')   seg1 = 091.
if (seg = 'BHB')   seg1 = 092.
if (seg = 'BHC')   seg1 = 093.
if (seg = 'BHD')   seg1 = 094.
if (seg = 'BHE')   seg1 = 095.
if (seg = 'BHF')   seg1 = 096.
if (seg = 'CAA')   seg1 = 097.
if (seg = 'CAB')   seg1 = 098.
if (seg = 'CAC')   seg1 = 099.
if (seg = 'CAD')   seg1 = 100.
if (seg = 'CAE')   seg1 = 101.
if (seg = 'CAF')   seg1 = 102.
if (seg = 'CBA')   seg1 = 103.
if (seg = 'CBB')   seg1 = 104.
if (seg = 'CBC')   seg1 = 105.
if (seg = 'CBD')   seg1 = 106.
if (seg = 'CBE')   seg1 = 107.
if (seg = 'CBF')   seg1 = 108.
if (seg = 'CCA')   seg1 = 109.
if (seg = 'CCB')   seg1 = 110.
if (seg = 'CCC')   seg1 = 111.
if (seg = 'CCD')   seg1 = 112.
if (seg = 'CCE')   seg1 = 113.
if (seg = 'CCF')   seg1 = 114.
if (seg = 'CDA')   seg1 = 115.
if (seg = 'CDB')   seg1 = 116.
if (seg = 'CDC')   seg1 = 117.
if (seg = 'CDD')   seg1 = 118.
if (seg = 'CDE')   seg1 = 119.
if (seg = 'CDF')   seg1 = 120.
if (seg = 'CEA')   seg1 = 121.
if (seg = 'CEB')   seg1 = 122.
if (seg = 'CEC')   seg1 = 123.
if (seg = 'CED')   seg1 = 124.
if (seg = 'CEE')   seg1 = 125.
if (seg = 'CEF')   seg1 = 126.
if (seg = 'CFA')   seg1 = 127.
if (seg = 'CFB')   seg1 = 128.
if (seg = 'CFC')   seg1 = 129.
if (seg = 'CFD')   seg1 = 130.
if (seg = 'CFE')   seg1 = 131.
if (seg = 'CFF')   seg1 = 132.
if (seg = 'CGA')   seg1 = 133.
if (seg = 'CGB')   seg1 = 134.
if (seg = 'CGC')   seg1 = 135.
if (seg = 'CGD')   seg1 = 136.
if (seg = 'CGE')   seg1 = 137.
if (seg = 'CGF')   seg1 = 138.
if (seg = 'CHA')   seg1 = 139.
if (seg = 'CHB')   seg1 = 140.
if (seg = 'CHC')   seg1 = 141.
if (seg = 'CHD')   seg1 = 142.
if (seg = 'CHE')   seg1 = 143.
if (seg = 'CHF')   seg1 = 144.
```

```
if (seg = 'DAA')  seg1 = 145.
if (seg = 'DAB')  seg1 = 146.
if (seg = 'DAC')  seg1 = 147.
if (seg = 'DAD')  seg1 = 148.
if (seg = 'DAE')  seg1 = 149.
if (seg = 'DAF')  seg1 = 150.
if (seg = 'DBA')  seg1 = 151.
if (seg = 'DBB')  seg1 = 152.
if (seg = 'DBC')  seg1 = 153.
if (seg = 'DBD')  seg1 = 154.
if (seg = 'DBE')  seg1 = 155.
if (seg = 'DBF')  seg1 = 156.
if (seg = 'DCA')  seg1 = 157.
if (seg = 'DCB')  seg1 = 158.
if (seg = 'DCC')  seg1 = 159.
if (seg = 'DCD')  seg1 = 160.
if (seg = 'DCE')  seg1 = 161.
if (seg = 'DCF')  seg1 = 162.
if (seg = 'DDA')  seg1 = 163.
if (seg = 'DDB')  seg1 = 164.
if (seg = 'DDC')  seg1 = 165.
if (seg = 'DDD')  seg1 = 166.
if (seg = 'DDE')  seg1 = 167.
if (seg = 'DDF')  seg1 = 168.
if (seg = 'DEA')  seg1 = 169.
if (seg = 'DEB')  seg1 = 170.
if (seg = 'DEC')  seg1 = 171.
if (seg = 'DED')  seg1 = 172.
if (seg = 'DEE')  seg1 = 173.
if (seg = 'DEF')  seg1 = 174.
if (seg = 'DFA')  seg1 = 175.
if (seg = 'DFB')  seg1 = 176.
if (seg = 'DFC')  seg1 = 177.
if (seg = 'DFD')  seg1 = 178.
if (seg = 'DFE')  seg1 = 179.
if (seg = 'DFF')  seg1 = 180.
if (seg = 'DGA')  seg1 = 181.
if (seg = 'DGB')  seg1 = 182.
if (seg = 'DGC')  seg1 = 183.
if (seg = 'DGD')  seg1 = 184.
if (seg = 'DGE')  seg1 = 185.
if (seg = 'DGF')  seg1 = 186.
if (seg = 'DHA')  seg1 = 187.
if (seg = 'DHB')  seg1 = 188.
if (seg = 'DHC')  seg1 = 189.
if (seg = 'DHD')  seg1 = 190.
if (seg = 'DHE')  seg1 = 191.
if (seg = 'DHF')  seg1 = 192.
if (seg = 'FAA')  seg1 = 193.
if (seg = 'FAB')  seg1 = 194.
if (seg = 'FAC')  seg1 = 195.
if (seg = 'FAD')  seg1 = 196.
if (seg = 'FAE')  seg1 = 197.
if (seg = 'FAF')  seg1 = 198.
if (seg = 'FBA')  seg1 = 199.
if (seg = 'FBB')  seg1 = 200.
if (seg = 'FBC')  seg1 = 201.
if (seg = 'FBD')  seg1 = 202.
if (seg = 'FBE')  seg1 = 203.
if (seg = 'FBF')  seg1 = 204.
if (seg = 'FCA')  seg1 = 205.
if (seg = 'FCB')  seg1 = 206.
if (seg = 'FCC')  seg1 = 207.
if (seg = 'FCD')  seg1 = 208.
if (seg = 'FCE')  seg1 = 209.
if (seg = 'FCF')  seg1 = 210.
if (seg = 'FDA')  seg1 = 211.
```

```
if (seg = 'FDB')   seg1 = 212.
if (seg = 'FDC')   seg1 = 213.
if (seg = 'FDD')   seg1 = 214.
if (seg = 'FDE')   seg1 = 215.
if (seg = 'FDF')   seg1 = 216.
if (seg = 'FEA')   seg1 = 217.
if (seg = 'FEB')   seg1 = 218.
if (seg = 'FEC')   seg1 = 219.
if (seg = 'FED')   seg1 = 220.
if (seg = 'FEE')   seg1 = 221.
if (seg = 'FEF')   seg1 = 222.
if (seg = 'FFA')   seg1 = 223.
if (seg = 'FFB')   seg1 = 224.
if (seg = 'FFC')   seg1 = 225.
if (seg = 'FFD')   seg1 = 226.
if (seg = 'FFE')   seg1 = 227.
if (seg = 'FFF')   seg1 = 228.
if (seg = 'FGA')   seg1 = 229.
if (seg = 'FGB')   seg1 = 230.
if (seg = 'FGC')   seg1 = 231.
if (seg = 'FGD')   seg1 = 232.
if (seg = 'FGE')   seg1 = 233.
if (seg = 'FGF')   seg1 = 234.
if (seg = 'FHA')   seg1 = 235.
if (seg = 'FHB')   seg1 = 236.
if (seg = 'FHC')   seg1 = 237.
if (seg = 'FHD')   seg1 = 238.
if (seg = 'FHE')   seg1 = 239.
if (seg = 'FHF')   seg1 = 240.
compute seg = gradef.
compute seg2 = 0.
if (seg = 'AAA')   seg2 = 001.
if (seg = 'AAB')   seg2 = 002.
if (seg = 'AAC')   seg2 = 003.
if (seg = 'AAD')   seg2 = 004.
if (seg = 'AAE')   seg2 = 005.
if (seg = 'AAF')   seg2 = 006.
if (seg = 'ABA')   seg2 = 007.
if (seg = 'ABB')   seg2 = 008.
if (seg = 'ABC')   seg2 = 009.
if (seg = 'ABD')   seg2 = 010.
if (seg = 'ABE')   seg2 = 011.
if (seg = 'ABF')   seg2 = 012.
if (seg = 'ACA')   seg2 = 013.
if (seg = 'ACB')   seg2 = 014.
if (seg = 'ACC')   seg2 = 015.
if (seg = 'ACD')   seg2 = 016.
if (seg = 'ACE')   seg2 = 017.
if (seg = 'ACF')   seg2 = 018.
if (seg = 'ADA')   seg2 = 019.
if (seg = 'ADB')   seg2 = 020.
if (seg = 'ADC')   seg2 = 021.
if (seg = 'ADD')   seg2 = 022.
if (seg = 'ADE')   seg2 = 023.
if (seg = 'ADF')   seg2 = 024.
if (seg = 'AEA')   seg2 = 025.
if (seg = 'AEB')   seg2 = 026.
if (seg = 'AEC')   seg2 = 027.
if (seg = 'AED')   seg2 = 028.
if (seg = 'AEE')   seg2 = 029.
if (seg = 'AEF')   seg2 = 030.
if (seg = 'AFA')   seg2 = 031.
if (seg = 'AFB')   seg2 = 032.
if (seg = 'AFC')   seg2 = 033.
if (seg = 'AFD')   seg2 = 034.
if (seg = 'AFE')   seg2 = 035.
if (seg = 'AFF')   seg2 = 036.
```

```
if (seg = 'AGA')   seg2 = 037.
if (seg = 'AGB')   seg2 = 038.
if (seg = 'AGC')   seg2 = 039.
if (seg = 'AGD')   seg2 = 040.
if (seg = 'AGE')   seg2 = 041.
if (seg = 'AGF')   seg2 = 042.
if (seg = 'AHA')   seg2 = 043.
if (seg = 'AHB')   seg2 = 044.
if (seg = 'AHC')   seg2 = 045.
if (seg = 'AHD')   seg2 = 046.
if (seg = 'AHE')   seg2 = 047.
if (seg = 'AHF')   seg2 = 048.
if (seg = 'BAA')   seg2 = 049.
if (seg = 'BAB')   seg2 = 050.
if (seg = 'BAC')   seg2 = 051.
if (seg = 'BAD')   seg2 = 052.
if (seg = 'BAE')   seg2 = 053.
if (seg = 'BAF')   seg2 = 054.
if (seg = 'BBA')   seg2 = 055.
if (seg = 'BBB')   seg2 = 056.
if (seg = 'BBC')   seg2 = 057.
if (seg = 'BBD')   seg2 = 058.
if (seg = 'BBE')   seg2 = 059.
if (seg = 'BBF')   seg2 = 060.
if (seg = 'BCA')   seg2 = 061.
if (seg = 'BCB')   seg2 = 062.
if (seg = 'BCC')   seg2 = 063.
if (seg = 'BCD')   seg2 = 064.
if (seg = 'BCE')   seg2 = 065.
if (seg = 'BCF')   seg2 = 066.
if (seg = 'BDA')   seg2 = 067.
if (seg = 'BDB')   seg2 = 068.
if (seg = 'BDC')   seg2 = 069.
if (seg = 'BDD')   seg2 = 070.
if (seg = 'BDE')   seg2 = 071.
if (seg = 'BDF')   seg2 = 072.
if (seg = 'BEA')   seg2 = 073.
if (seg = 'BEB')   seg2 = 074.
if (seg = 'BEC')   seg2 = 075.
if (seg = 'BED')   seg2 = 076.
if (seg = 'BEE')   seg2 = 077.
if (seg = 'BEF')   seg2 = 078.
if (seg = 'BFA')   seg2 = 079.
if (seg = 'BFB')   seg2 = 080.
if (seg = 'BFC')   seg2 = 081.
if (seg = 'BFD')   seg2 = 082.
if (seg = 'BFE')   seg2 = 083.
if (seg = 'BFF')   seg2 = 084.
if (seg = 'BGA')   seg2 = 085.
if (seg = 'BGB')   seg2 = 086.
if (seg = 'BGC')   seg2 = 087.
if (seg = 'BGD')   seg2 = 088.
if (seg = 'BGE')   seg2 = 089.
if (seg = 'BGF')   seg2 = 090.
if (seg = 'BHA')   seg2 = 091.
if (seg = 'BHB')   seg2 = 092.
if (seg = 'BHC')   seg2 = 093.
if (seg = 'BHD')   seg2 = 094.
if (seg = 'BHE')   seg2 = 095.
if (seg = 'BHF')   seg2 = 096.
if (seg = 'CAA')   seg2 = 097.
if (seg = 'CAB')   seg2 = 098.
if (seg = 'CAC')   seg2 = 099.
if (seg = 'CAD')   seg2 = 100.
if (seg = 'CAE')   seg2 = 101.
if (seg = 'CAF')   seg2 = 102.
if (seg = 'CBA')   seg2 = 103.
```

```
if (seg = 'CBB')   seg2 = 104.
if (seg = 'CBC')   seg2 = 105.
if (seg = 'CBD')   seg2 = 106.
if (seg = 'CBE')   seg2 = 107.
if (seg = 'CBF')   seg2 = 108.
if (seg = 'CCA')   seg2 = 109.
if (seg = 'CCB')   seg2 = 110.
if (seg = 'CCC')   seg2 = 111.
if (seg = 'CCD')   seg2 = 112.
if (seg = 'CCE')   seg2 = 113.
if (seg = 'CCF')   seg2 = 114.
if (seg = 'CDA')   seg2 = 115.
if (seg = 'CDB')   seg2 = 116.
if (seg = 'CDC')   seg2 = 117.
if (seg = 'CDD')   seg2 = 118.
if (seg = 'CDE')   seg2 = 119.
if (seg = 'CDF')   seg2 = 120.
if (seg = 'CEA')   seg2 = 121.
if (seg = 'CEB')   seg2 = 122.
if (seg = 'CEC')   seg2 = 123.
if (seg = 'CED')   seg2 = 124.
if (seg = 'CEE')   seg2 = 125.
if (seg = 'CEF')   seg2 = 126.
if (seg = 'CFA')   seg2 = 127.
if (seg = 'CFB')   seg2 = 128.
if (seg = 'CFC')   seg2 = 129.
if (seg = 'CFD')   seg2 = 130.
if (seg = 'CFE')   seg2 = 131.
if (seg = 'CFF')   seg2 = 132.
if (seg = 'CGA')   seg2 = 133.
if (seg = 'CGB')   seg2 = 134.
if (seg = 'CGC')   seg2 = 135.
if (seg = 'CGD')   seg2 = 136.
if (seg = 'CGE')   seg2 = 137.
if (seg = 'CGF')   seg2 = 138.
if (seg = 'CHA')   seg2 = 139.
if (seg = 'CHB')   seg2 = 140.
if (seg = 'CHC')   seg2 = 141.
if (seg = 'CHD')   seg2 = 142.
if (seg = 'CHE')   seg2 = 143.
if (seg = 'CHF')   seg2 = 144.
if (seg = 'DAA')   seg2 = 145.
if (seg = 'DAB')   seg2 = 146.
if (seg = 'DAC')   seg2 = 147.
if (seg = 'DAD')   seg2 = 148.
if (seg = 'DAE')   seg2 = 149.
if (seg = 'DAF')   seg2 = 150.
if (seg = 'DBA')   seg2 = 151.
if (seg = 'DBB')   seg2 = 152.
if (seg = 'DBC')   seg2 = 153.
if (seg = 'DBD')   seg2 = 154.
if (seg = 'DBE')   seg2 = 155.
if (seg = 'DBF')   seg2 = 156.
if (seg = 'DCA')   seg2 = 157.
if (seg = 'DCB')   seg2 = 158.
if (seg = 'DCC')   seg2 = 159.
if (seg = 'DCD')   seg2 = 160.
if (seg = 'DCE')   seg2 = 161.
if (seg = 'DCF')   seg2 = 162.
if (seg = 'DDA')   seg2 = 163.
if (seg = 'DDB')   seg2 = 164.
if (seg = 'DDC')   seg2 = 165.
if (seg = 'DDD')   seg2 = 166.
if (seg = 'DDE')   seg2 = 167.
if (seg = 'DDF')   seg2 = 168.
if (seg = 'DEA')   seg2 = 169.
if (seg = 'DEB')   seg2 = 170.
```

```
if (seg = 'DEC')   seg2 = 171.
if (seg = 'DED')   seg2 = 172.
if (seg = 'DEE')   seg2 = 173.
if (seg = 'DEF')   seg2 = 174.
if (seg = 'DFA')   seg2 = 175.
if (seg = 'DFB')   seg2 = 176.
if (seg = 'DFC')   seg2 = 177.
if (seg = 'DFD')   seg2 = 178.
if (seg = 'DFE')   seg2 = 179.
if (seg = 'DFF')   seg2 = 180.
if (seg = 'DGA')   seg2 = 181.
if (seg = 'DGB')   seg2 = 182.
if (seg = 'DGC')   seg2 = 183.
if (seg = 'DGD')   seg2 = 184.
if (seg = 'DGE')   seg2 = 185.
if (seg = 'DGF')   seg2 = 186.
if (seg = 'DHA')   seg2 = 187.
if (seg = 'DHB')   seg2 = 188.
if (seg = 'DHC')   seg2 = 189.
if (seg = 'DHD')   seg2 = 190.
if (seg = 'DHE')   seg2 = 191.
if (seg = 'DHF')   seg2 = 192.
if (seg = 'FAA')   seg2 = 193.
if (seg = 'FAB')   seg2 = 194.
if (seg = 'FAC')   seg2 = 195.
if (seg = 'FAD')   seg2 = 196.
if (seg = 'FAE')   seg2 = 197.
if (seg = 'FAF')   seg2 = 198.
if (seg = 'FBA')   seg2 = 199.
if (seg = 'FBB')   seg2 = 200.
if (seg = 'FBC')   seg2 = 201.
if (seg = 'FBD')   seg2 = 202.
if (seg = 'FBE')   seg2 = 203.
if (seg = 'FBF')   seg2 = 204.
if (seg = 'FCA')   seg2 = 205.
if (seg = 'FCB')   seg2 = 206.
if (seg = 'FCC')   seg2 = 207.
if (seg = 'FCD')   seg2 = 208.
if (seg = 'FCE')   seg2 = 209.
if (seg = 'FCF')   seg2 = 210.
if (seg = 'FDA')   seg2 = 211.
if (seg = 'FDB')   seg2 = 212.
if (seg = 'FDC')   seg2 = 213.
if (seg = 'FDD')   seg2 = 214.
if (seg = 'FDE')   seg2 = 215.
if (seg = 'FDF')   seg2 = 216.
if (seg = 'FEA')   seg2 = 217.
if (seg = 'FEB')   seg2 = 218.
if (seg = 'FEC')   seg2 = 219.
if (seg = 'FED')   seg2 = 220.
if (seg = 'FEE')   seg2 = 221.
if (seg = 'FEF')   seg2 = 222.
if (seg = 'FFA')   seg2 = 223.
if (seg = 'FFB')   seg2 = 224.
if (seg = 'FFC')   seg2 = 225.
if (seg = 'FFD')   seg2 = 226.
if (seg = 'FFE')   seg2 = 227.
if (seg = 'FFF')   seg2 = 228.
if (seg = 'FGA')   seg2 = 229.
if (seg = 'FGB')   seg2 = 230.
if (seg = 'FGC')   seg2 = 231.
if (seg = 'FGD')   seg2 = 232.
if (seg = 'FGE')   seg2 = 233.
if (seg = 'FGF')   seg2 = 234.
if (seg = 'FHA')   seg2 = 235.
if (seg = 'FHB')   seg2 = 236.
if (seg = 'FHC')   seg2 = 237.
```

```
if (seg = 'FHD')   seg2 = 238.
if (seg = 'FHE')   seg2 = 239.
if (seg = 'FHF')   seg2 = 240.
aggregate outfile = 'c:\datasets\dummy8.sav'
         /break          = seg2
         /cases          = n.
*** Adjust For New Customers *****************.
select if (seg1 = 999) or (gradep = 'ZZZZZZ').
compute seg2 = seg2 + 300.
formats seg1(f3.0) seg2(f3.0).
aggregate outfile = *
         /break          = seg2
         /cases          = n.
add files  file = 'c:\datasets\dummy8.sav'
           /file = *.
execute.
save outfile = 'c:\datasets\dummy8.sav'.
execute.
*** Make Sure That 0 Populated Cells Count ***.
get file = 'c:\datasets\dummy2.sav'.
compute seg2 = order.
formats seg2(f8.0).
save outfile = 'c:\datasets\dummy9.sav'
         /keep = seg2.
execute.
compute seg2 = seg2 + 300.
add files  file = 'c:\datasets\dummy9.sav'
           /file = *
           /keep = seg2.
match files  file = *
             /file = 'c:\datasets\dummy8.sav'
             /by = seg2.
formats seg2(f8.0) cases(f8.0).
if missing(cases)  cases = 0.
execute.
save outfile = 'c:\datasets\dummy9.sav'.
execute.
*** Now We Need To Calculate Rebuy Rates To Plug Into The Spreadsheet ***.
add files  file = 'c:\datasets\dummy6.sav'
           /file = 'c:\datasets\dummy7.sav'.
sort cases by rebuy.
sort cases by seg1.
compute buyer = 0.
compute nonbuyer = 0.
if (rebuy = 0)  nonbuyer = cases.
if (rebuy = 1)  buyer = cases.
compute seg2 = seg1.
aggregate outfile = *
         /break          = seg2
         /buyer          = sum(buyer)
         /nonbuyer       = sum(nonbuyer).
compute rebuy = 0.
if (buyer + nonbuyer > 0)  rebuy = (buyer) / (buyer + nonbuyer).
if (seg2 ge 300)  rebuy = 1.
formats seg2(f3.0) rebuy(f6.4).
match files  file = 'c:\datasets\dummy9.sav'
             /file = *
             /by = seg2
             /keep = seg2 cases rebuy.
execute.
```

Contact Information:

Kevin Hillstrom
President, MineThatData
E-Mail: kevinh@minethatdata.com
Website: http://minethatdata.com
Blog: http://minethatdata.com/blog
Twitter: http://twitter.com/minethatdata

4753929R00088

Made in the USA
San Bernardino, CA
05 October 2013